DATE DUE

JY 22 99		
FE 10 00		
AP 2 07		

DEMCO 38-296

"I have been using Buying Facilitation for two years. . . . My business has increased dramatically; I work more effectively with higher quality skills, more excitement, and more time off than ever before; my personal communication has improved dramatically; and my excitement with my work continues growing as a result. Where was this new sales paradigm during all those years I struggled with sales?"

—Carolyn Gold, President, The Gold Group

"Morgen's no-nonsense, common-sense approach to sales puts the customer in the position of controlling the purchase process, based on his/her need to buy, not on the sellers need to sell. And that is a major step toward customer comfort and delight. Creating such a 'comfort zone' with the customer is critical to the business of telephone sales and service. As such, I look for these techniques to be adopted on a wide scale throughout the telebusiness sector. Indeed, I would hope that everyone in a sales position would take note."

—Robert E. Van Voohris, Jr., Editor-in-Chief, *Teleprofessional Magazine*

"Morgen offers a dramatically new paradigm for selling which has evolved from her own sales experience. She clearly positions her 'Buying Facilitation' approach in relation to mainstream selling methods and offers regular opportunities for self-assessment. In her step-by-step exposition, Sharon Drew looks in depth at the core of selling skills and how to develop them."

—John Adams, Executive Education Program Manager, Sun Microsystems, Inc.

"**Sharon Drew Morgen brought an innovative approach** to our dynamic marketing center and our technology-based clients. The results of her methodology surpassed all other training programs used in our years of experience as one of the largest telephone sales companies in the country. The Morgen Buying Facilitation Method increased program sales over 200% of our current run rate and greatly reduced the length of our sales cycle. Our salespeople were happier also."

—Laura Schaeffer, General Manager, The Southerland Group, Inc.

"**With Buying Facilitation, I have increased my revenue dramatically** while selling ethically and maintaining long-term client relations. I use Buying Facilitation throughout the sales cycle and for customer service. It's the best method I've ever used."

—Nick Miller, President, Clarity Advantage

"**Most 'how-to-sell' books are either fluffy** ('be aggressive'), gimmicky ('make sure you have a pleasant voice'), or manipulative ('tell the secretary you know the boss'), because the authors don't understand (or believe) that selling is actually about helping customers help themselves toward finding their own most workable solutions . . . . Sharon Drew's work is revolutionary, practical, curiously simple, and above all, amazingly effective."

—Michael Fulenwider, President, Multimedia Associates

SELLING WITH
INTEGRITY

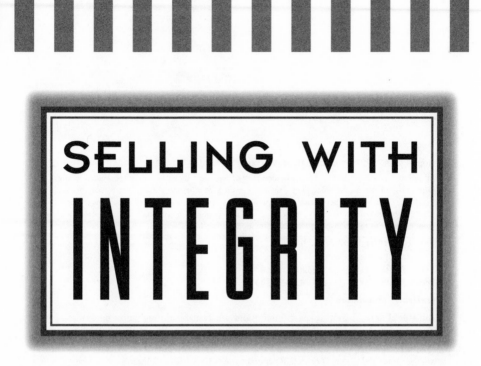

SELLING WITH
INTEGRITY

REINVENTING SALES
THROUGH COLLABORATION,
RESPECT, AND SERVING

SHARON DREW MORGEN

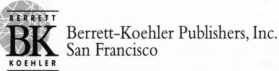

Berrett-Koehler Publishers, Inc.
San Francisco

Berrett-Koehler Publishers, Inc.
450 Sansome Street, Suite 1200
San Francisco, CA 94111-3320
Tel: 415-288-0260   Fax: 415-362-2512

Ordering Information

Individual sales. Berrett-Koehler publications are available through most bookstores. They can also be ordered direct from Berrett-Koehler at the address above.

Quantity sales. Special discounts are available on quantity purchases by corporations, associations, and others. For details, contact the "Special Sales Department" at the Berrett-Koehler address above.

Orders for college textbook/course adoption use. Please contact Berrett-Koehler Publishers at the address above.

Orders by U.S. trade bookstores and wholesalers. Please contact Publishers Group West, 4065 Hollis Street, Box 8843, Emeryville, CA 94662; 510-658-3453; 1-800-788-3123.

Printed in the United States of America

 Printed on acid-free and recycled paper that is composed of 50% recovered fiber, including 10% postconsumer waste.

Library of Congress Cataloging-in-Publication Data
Morgen, Sharon Drew, 1946–
    Selling with integrity : reinventing sales through collaboration, respect, and serving / Sharon Drew Morgen.
        p.   cm.
    ISBN 1–57675–015–9 (alk. paper)
    1. Selling—Moral and ethical aspects.   2. Integrity.
HF5438.25.M665   1997
658.85—dc21   96–53215
                                                                     CIP

First Edition
01 00 99 98 97   10 9 8 7 6 5 4 3 2 1

All rights to the service mark for The Morgen Buying Facilitation Method are the property of Morgen Facilitations, Inc.

Copyeditor: Mary Lou Sumberg
Text designer: Detta Penna

*Dedicated to all sellers
who believe it is possible
to bring their hearts to work.*

The ultimate purpose of business is not,
or should not be, simply to make money.
Nor is it merely a system of making and selling things.
The promise of business is to increase
the general well-being of humankind through service,
a creative invention and ethical philosophy.

—Paul Hawken
The Ecology of Commerce

Table of Contents

CHAPTER 10 Formulating the Right Questions   135

CHAPTER 11 Listening Skills   153

III   Being a Buying Facilitator   167

CHAPTER 12 Using Buying Facilitation: Putting the
            Skills Together   169

CHAPTER 13 Strengthening Customer Service
            through Buying Facilitation   181

CHAPTER 14 Case Comparisons: Buying Facilitation,
            Traditional Sales, and Consultative Sales   187

CHAPTER 15 Managing Salespeople in a
            Buying Facilitation Environment   195

CHAPTER 16 Buying Facilitation in Action: On-the-Phone,
            Face-to-Face, and Across Sales Contexts   205

CHAPTER 17 Reinventing Business by Reinventing Sales   221

            Appendix   227

            Bibliography   231

            Index   233

            About the Author   241

Foreword

Throughout most of the long history of sales, there has often been an adversarial relationship between sellers and buyers. Why? Sellers have historically been charged with the task of convincing . . . by any means necessary . . . the buyers to part with as much of their money as possible . . . often without regard to what is needed by those buyers. Hence the oft-quoted phrase *Caveat Emptor* (buyer beware), which might well be equated with yard signs that say *Beware of Dog*.

In the early days, despite some degree of mistrust, the arrival of the salesman was a welcome event. Why? Because he was a primary, if not sole, supplier of needed goods. So even though buyers might not trust him completely, that slight fault was overlooked in light of the value provided.

But in today's world, there are a plethora of vendors from which a buyer can choose. This in turn creates greater competition for the buyer's money, forcing sales people to resort to even more aggressive tactics.

Little wonder, then, that sales people too often treat buyers like sheep to be fleeced. Less wonder that buyers resist. In this era of distance selling (via telephone, mail, Internet, whatever), the buyers' learned mistrust of the sales process has created additional hurdles which must be cleared before a sale can be consummated. It is more difficult for a seller to impose his or her personal charms on the buyer, so the sales message is more easily discounted and/or ignored. In addition, too many less-than-scrupulously-honest sales people and/or companies have made the buyers even more wary of "being sold."

I first became acquainted with Sharon Drew Morgen several years ago when she called and said she had an article that I might like to publish, but that I should be aware that it might well offend some of our readers as it condemned most currently used telephone sales techniques. I found that material a refreshing change from much that was published on the subject, as well as feeling that it fit well with the changing times and a move toward the then-infant concept of "relationship selling." Time has proven that judgement correct and the world is coming to an understanding that the concepts Sharon Drew has been discussing are invaluable, if not necessary, as an aid to breaking down the barriers between buyer and seller.

Unfortunately, the basic concept behind Sharon Drew's selling technique is so simple that it seems to have eluded most everyone, and therein lies the shame. In the past, many "sales gurus" have promulgated rigid, formulaic processes that "guarantee" sales results. Unfortunately for us all, many actually have worked, which in the long run has only tended to make buyers even more wary of salespeople and their crafty ways.

Sharon Drew's no-nonsense, common-sense approach to sales puts the customer in the position of controlling the purchase process, based on his or her need to buy, not the salesperson's need to sell. And that is a major step toward the "customer comfort and delight" that is the goal of most sales and service programs today. In my area of business (telephone sales, service, and support), creating such a "comfort zone" for the customer is critical to continued industry growth. It will soon become recognized as increasingly important for all avenues of sales, from the most complex sales cycle, down to the simple retail purchase level. As such, I look for these tactics to be adopted on a wide scale throughout all business sectors, but especially within call centers. Indeed, I would hope that everyone in a sales-related position would take note. Wouldn't it be nice not to dread the sales person?

Robert E. Van Voorhis, Jr., Editor-in-Chief
TeleProfessional Magazine

Preface

Some years ago, I made several life-changing discoveries that gave me the ability to incorporate my personal spiritual values into my job of selling. As a result, I designed a sales methodology I call Buying Facilitation.

For eleven years I have used this methodology successfully, both as a seller and as an entrepreneur, and have developed it into a replicable system. For the past seven years I have been teaching it—in mom-and-pop operations as well as Fortune 500 companies—to salespeople, teams, and departments who have been seeking a sales methodology more in line with their principles and values. Buying Facilitation is now well tested, and it is time to share it with a wider audience.

Why I Wrote This Book

Selling with Integrity is designed to assist you in aligning your beliefs, skills, and behaviors with your personal principles and spiritual values; it will also help you bring your personal principles and values to the sales arena. For me, living my spiritual values means I choose to live my life in creative support of the earth and each person I encounter, and I take responsibility to honor each person's uniqueness while offering communications with honesty, integrity, and respect. As a seller, these are the values I work with:

Interdependence: Working in collaboration brings more meaningful interactions with prospects and clients, which creates efficient problem solving, loyalty, and interdependence over time.

Empowerment: Assuming buyers have their own answers supports trusting interactions, ending the rejection and objections caused when we assume we know the answers for another.

Service: Taking the responsibility to assist prospects in sequentially ordering their thinking around how to meet their needs with existent resources whenever possible creates a serving environment.

Respect and Trust: Creating and maintaining rapport, trust, and relationship develops a collaboration which lays the foundation to assist buyers to quickly discern what, if anything, they need to buy and subsequently leads to more closed sales and easily met quotas.

It is by aligning your behaviors with values such as the above that you can sell in a way that has integrity—both for the buyer and the seller. Until now, sales methodologies have not taught sellers how to take responsibility to assist buyers in sequentially ordering their thinking to help them help themselves—*with the belief that the buyer, not the seller, has the answers, and that the sales process promotes discovery, not product.*

In fact, in Buying Facilitation, selling the product is one possible solution, not the goal, since each prospect has her own answers dependent upon her job, her resources, her teammates, and the political and financial issues surrounding the identified problem. The seller becomes responsible for creating an environment of support and discovery in which both seller and prospect get their needs met.

How to Use
This Book

I have organized this book into three sections, in the sequence of beliefs, skills, and behaviors. What is the difference between a belief, a skill, and a behavior?

Beliefs are the values and principles with which we assess the world. The stated beliefs in this book are based on the spiritual values I've described and how they relate to a selling environment. Throughout the book you will note a strong focus on underlying beliefs; I believe it is easier to change behavior if beliefs have changed first. The basic beliefs of Buying Facilitation are presented in Section I.

Skills are the actual components of how to do something; they are the tools that bridge your beliefs and behaviors. As an example, in *Selling with Integrity* I break down listening, question formulation, and observing into learnable and replicable chunks, so you can consciously choose the approaches most appropriate for a given situation. The skills are presented in Section II.

Behaviors are the methods and techniques used to implement the skills and beliefs. So while you learn the skill of question formulation, the actual behavior would be to ask a question. The implementation of Buying Facilitation is presented in Section III.

I believe anyone in the sales profession, as well as in customer service, will benefit from the beliefs, skills, and behaviors offered in this book. Specifically, I have geared the book toward business-to-business sales—including prospecting, qualifying, cold calling, face-to-face visits, follow-up visits, and problem solving. Many of the examples I've provided are qualifying dialogues because they are the best examples for learning the intricacies of the new method. I've also included a chapter on customer service.

Buying Facilitation applies to a wide range of situations and selling environments, however, because it is a methodology based on a communication approach, not a specific selling style. As a result, retail sellers and telemarketers in consumer-based sales will find the skills useful, also. Any environment will benefit from communication based on a seller consciously choosing to take responsibility to support an environment of discovery.

To take into account the fact that both men and women work in sales, I have alternated the use of masculine and feminine pronouns by chapter.

Learning through Practice

Throughout the book I have provided Skill Sets to aid your learning. Buying Facilitation is a methodology very different from sales as you've known it, with different beliefs, skills, and behaviors from either Traditional or Consultative sales methodologies. It is important to have a dedicated approach to learning it. It is most effective to work with the Skill Sets by writing down your responses to them in a learning journal that you can reread.

The Skill Sets will lead you to recognize your current sales beliefs and behaviors in relation to the new ones put forth, and offer you practice in learning those skills that might improve your selling. Since I cannot be there to teach you directly, I offer you personal practice through them. They are not easy, but they will push your learning curve immensely.

I believe change takes place when beliefs and behaviors align. It is therefore necessary to understand the way you sell now and how that relates to your current values and beliefs. I have included as much hands-on practical learning as possible, and hope you will find some of the more technical information—how specifically to listen, for example—helpful.

Haven't I Been Doing This Already?

I offer this methodology with some caution, however. It's not that what you have been doing is wrong: just that there are additional choices you can make to supplement your current skills, to help where the skills and behaviors you've been using have not been giving you the results you wish.

I believe that a majority of sellers, using their unique selling skills and whatever sales approaches they select, prefer to approach a buyer with an attitude of service and respect. In fact, sales gurus, from Carnegie to Zigler to Rackham and Sandler and Tracy, have always taught that the customer deserves to be respected and honored. Additionally, with few exceptions, every seller I've ever met ultimately believes she's serving her customers. But there has been an incongruence between the beliefs, the skills, and the application.

Other sales methodologies haven't gone as far as we need them to go to bring the actual how-tos of the beliefs based on serving down to the behavioral level. I am suggesting that we need to go further at this point in history, and I am delighted to offer you Buying Facilitation. I look forward to offering you what I've learned to assist you in aligning your values, ethics, and principles with a successful sales career. I know it will bring you a happier workday, loyal clients, easy prospecting sessions, and most of all, congruence between your personal values and your career. You *can* make money and sell with integrity.

Sharon Drew Morgen
Taos, New Mexico
January 1997

Acknowledgments

Since I was a girl, I've lived with the hope that people would speak to each other respectfully and treat each other as if they each mattered.

I have grown through life determined and dedicated to doing my share to make the skills available, if only to provide a safe place for myself.

Many people have taught me the skills I've needed to use personally and professionally, without which I wouldn't be the person who could discover this model.

For assisting me in gaining the personal skills necessary to be available to learn my lessons, I'd like to thank Sara Frank, Richard Travis, Nikki Yeracaris, Alexandra Karan, Wayne Muller, Stan Grov, Jack Kornfield, Joseph Goldstein, Sharon Salzberg, Gene Early, Robert Dilts, Eileen Watkins-Seymour, Graham Dawes.

Others believed in me when I had about given up on myself: Barbara Marx Hubbard, Jeffrey Mishlove, Willis Harman, Michael Ray, Jeff Hutner, Dave Heil, Marilee Goldberg, BJ Hateley, Bob Van Voohris, and Denise Anderson.

The people who showed up to help me garner my skills and put them into a method were my angels. I deeply thank Linda Burgess and DeAnne Rosenberg.

I would like to thank all of my clients, who trusted and supported me, often in the face of corporate distrust and doubt.

I would like to thank my neighbors and Native American

friends in Taos, New Mexico, who supported me through my discovery of self.

And finally, the two people who pushed and cajoled me with deep respect, grace, and humor through this writing process, who helped me "come out" and own my spiritual connection with my sales methodology, which is the true gift of this book, Steven Piersanti and Alis Valencia.

Thank you all for helping me be all I can be.

And a special thanks to the Creator who gave me this wonderful model to share with the world. I am humbly grateful for the chance to serve.

I

A New Relationship-Based, Solution-Focused Sales Approach

In this section, we will explore how a new relationship-based, solution-focused sales approach was discovered and how it differs from Traditional and Consultative sales methodologies in relation to beliefs, skills, responsibilities, and principles. We will also look at how this sales approach fits in with the other new paradigm thinking in business today.

Because it's such a new way to sell, I've included examples to help you with your everyday tasks.

Chapter 1

The Buyer Taught Me How to Sell

I didn't go about creating a new sales methodology on purpose. In fact,

It Began by Accident

In 1984, my former husband, Ben, and I went to England to work for an international computer services company. His job was a highly technical field job, mine an in-house sales management position following years on Wall Street as a stockbroker. After just a few days, I knew the job I had accepted was not for me, and I spoke to the vice president offering to resign. The company allowed me to create my own job rather than have me leave and take their new technical guru with me. The parameters they offered gave me freedom to experiment. Since this new position wasn't budgeted for, they would pay me a percentage of gross profits rather than a salary.

I designed a job to support the type of work my husband was doing. Since I heard him complain regularly that there was nowhere for companies to go for systems design, or training support in the Fourth Generation Language (4GL) arena he was working in, it made sense to me that there was a service to provide and money to be made. The problem was that I didn't quite understand what I was to be selling. Try as he might, Ben—with his overdeveloped left brain—couldn't get me to understand fully what was needed on the technical end. With my overdeveloped right brain, I saw all the implications, the possibilities, the interrelationships of people to computers to jobs—I just didn't get exactly what I would be selling.

To begin with, the idea wasn't fully formed. As I discovered people's needs, I knew I'd have the flexibility to create a service that would support them. Since I didn't have a complete picture of what was possible, however, I hadn't a clue what that service might be or what would have to happen from my end to create that service. Secondly, I didn't know how I'd notice any needs or sound intelligent enough to sell something I didn't have.

None of this bothered me. I didn't take the job seriously. Ben had only a six-month commitment and plenty of salary. I wasn't actually getting paid. We were in Europe and could travel to Paris or Naples or wherever on weekends. I looked at it as a great vacation, and figured I could look busy for a few months. I could even have some fun learning how to do business in a foreign country. I did have a sense of challenge, however: I was a seasoned, successful salesperson; I knew I could sell anything if I could sell myself. I decided to give it a try.

In my tiny office, I picked up the Yellow Pages and went to the As. Because it was an American company, American Express sounded manageable.

I called the receptionist. When I heard her voice, I immediately broke out into a sweat: What was I going to say? What was I selling? Merrill Lynch, EFHutton, and Kidder Peabody had taught me to go into each call knowing my outcome, knowing my product, and knowing how to take control of the sales situation. But here I was, in a strange country, selling a product as yet unformed, and if I'm to be honest, not understood.

"American Express. Can I help you?"

"Oh, hello. My name is Sharon Drew Morgen. I'm sure you're busy, but I'm wondering if you'd have a few moments to help me."

I knew I needed help—lots of help. I was trying to be nice, to get into some kind of rapport given all that I wanted from her.

"Sure, I'll try. And if I get busy you can call me back. How can I help?" I was relieved. A nice person who wanted to help.

"I'm new to the U.K. and am starting up a computer support services company. (I hoped she knew what that meant; I didn't.) I'm wondering if there are any specific people at American Express who take care of your computer support needs?" I didn't have a clue who or what job description to ask for. The best I could do was to rely on her help and knowledge.

"We have several groups who do that. Let me give you some names and numbers. If you need more, call me back and I'll see what else I can do for you. Good luck." I felt lucky already.

I called the first person on the list.

"Hi. This is Jim."

"Hi. This is Sharon Drew Morgen. This is a sales call. Is this a good time to speak?" I needed patience and time. I was hoping by letting him know it was a sales call and by asking about any time constraints, he'd have both the patience and time I'd need.

Jim broke out into laughter. "That's great. What are you selling?"

"I hear you have time to speak. Is that true?"

"It depends on what you're selling. But you've intrigued me already. What's up?"

"I'm starting up a computer support services company working with Fourth Generation Languages. Do you deal with that in your job?"

"I try to."

"Since I'm so new—you're my first call actually—I'm trying to put together a group of services that would support you." (I didn't really say anything here. Maybe he would understand this vague description.) "Would you mind if I asked you some questions to see if we're in the same arena?" I was hoping to get an understanding of what a 4GL environment looked like, maybe get a sense of what might be missing, and maybe get clever and come up with something to sell him. Then all I'd need to do would be to create it.

"I'd be glad to."

I began asking him questions about the specifics of his current environment. I figured if he could take a good look around and see clearly everything going on, he'd be able to see what was missing and tell me what he needed to buy. He began telling me about his hardware, software, and staffing. I had to keep interjecting questions to keep the chunks small, since I didn't really understand him if he gave me too much information at once.

I felt seriously stupid. The best I could do was use the information he was giving me to formulate the next questions since I didn't even know what to base questions on. Every once in a while I summarized what he'd said in order to keep myself on the right track.

I didn't get into the content of his situation since I wouldn't have understood it anyway, so I listened for areas in his thinking that made me feel incomplete, and then carefully asked questions in those areas. It was easy to formulate questions based on the information Jim was giving me as I didn't have anything of my own to direct the conversation around.

During my questioning, I noticed Jim got really thoughtful about some of the situations he was facing. He seemed to use the questions as a way to look at his culture through new eyes: he put some themes together and rejected others. He juxtaposed internal problems and solutions. He played with possibilities he'd not thought of before. And I kept asking questions with the assumption—the hope, in fact—that he had all the pieces in place to solve his own problems.

We got to a point where Jim discovered he was missing some specific technical support. Since I didn't know how to fix his problem but obviously couldn't tell him that, I asked him if American Express could fix it for him. He thought about it and realized they probably could.

As the call ended, Jim thanked me for leading him through a discovery process that gave him information in advance of a problem, and for helping him to help himself with a solution. He kindly gave me more names to call, some from other companies.

I got off the call in shock. It worked. Whatever I'd done, I'd managed to help someone find a problem and a solution, and I even got referrals. In addition, I was very happy I didn't have to sell anything since I had no idea what I would have sold.

I now had a bunch of names to start calling. For the next several weeks, I followed this process:

1. Get into rapport with the receptionist/secretary and get whatever help she could offer.

2. Get into rapport with the prospective buyer and let him know this was a sales call so he would know the parameters and rules of our interaction.

3. Use questions to take a look at where the buyer was and where he was going to see if anything was missing.

4. Elicit the aid of the buyer's teammates as well as his company's expertise to see if he could discover how to help himself with his problem.

5. Get referrals if internal solutions were available and no external support was needed.

Eventually, some of the people I called discovered they needed some external services. Generally, when they discovered internal solutions would not solve their problems, they looked to me for answers, but only when they realized their internal resources were inadequate.

In the beginning, I didn't have any answers. So I led the prospects through another stage of questions so they could specifically discover what their answers would look like. The questions I asked elicited information from them in regard to choosing solutions. They had to go through another discovery process to ascertain specifically what it was they needed to buy, how they wanted to buy, what it would look like, and what criteria it had to meet for their decision-making team.

New pieces were added to my initial process:

6. Assist in determining all the criteria for bringing in an external resource that would satisfy the culture/team/decision-making body once it was acknowledged that there were inadequate internal resources.

7. Facilitate the discovery of how they would know that what I provided was what they were seeking (i.e., how would they know they would want to buy something from me?).

8. Collaborate to decide how to go forward together.

I asked questions to give prospects the best shot at discovering their specific needs. Because the answers were so specific and because I was in such a unique situation of being able to create (with Ben's patient help) what was necessary, business started coming in. All I really had to do was create the solution they discovered.

As I got busier, I also got smarter. I began knowing what people wanted. I wasn't stupid any more. It felt great to know what I was selling and be able to take control of the conversation and the sales situation. I began using the sales techniques I'd learned in previous sales training programs. "Oh, I could do that for you," I'd say. "Here's what you need." Or "Don't you think you should be looking at *this* type of a solution?"

Business started falling off. I couldn't imagine why. I finally knew my product, knew how to position it, and knew how to control the conversation so I'd be in the best position to convince my prospect that what I had and what he needed matched. But there was no new incoming business.

One day my first prospect, Jim, called and ordered $150,000 worth of services.

"But you didn't need me." I was surprised.

"Well, I thought American Express could take care of everything for me. But when the time came, there were no consultants available. And those questions you made me answer got me thinking of other areas that needed problem solving. Can you help out?"

At that point I realized that all the sales training I'd received was based on how and what I sold. Jim taught me that no matter how much or how little I knew about my product or about selling, I would have had nothing to sell if there was no one to buy.

I went back to being stupid, to asking questions that helped prospective buyers discover how best to get their own needs met, trusting they had their own answers. My business grew to $5,000,000 in revenue within four years.

And since I was having so much fun, being so creative, and making so much money, I decided to stay in England.

I Thought I Knew How to Sell

To be honest, it was a bit of a shock. I had learned to sell on Wall Street. My colleagues and clients were tough, fast moving, and only wanted answers. Quickly. I had to know my product and have my sales skills down pat. Smile and dial. Come in with a great opening. Wow them with sexy stocks and great numbers. Be clever and charming, and let the buyer think he was calling the shots. Wow him with some great ideas for stocks, then call back after those stocks had gone up so he'd open an account. Don't call back if the stock was a loser. Call your client just often enough, but not too much or he'll think you don't have any other clients. Ask for referrals, but only after you made him money. Let each client think he was the only one.

I was good. I had a great opening gambit:

"Hi, Mr. Jones. I'm Sharon Drew Morgen with Merrill Lynch and I'm a broker. I'd like to take three and one-half minutes of your time to tell you about a stock that's going to go up in the next week. Do you want to make some money? Or maybe just watch it for the week so you'll know if I'm worth my salt? Got the time?"

I was trained by the best. I made money. I had clients. And I never would have known there was a better way, a way that *served* me and my clients *and* made me more money, until I backed into it in England.

If I had known what I was selling, I never would have considered asking uninformed questions in order to get a prospective buyer to decide whether or not his existing resources were adequate or to sequentially order his thinking to discern all of the pieces of the problem with their potential solutions. I would have believed it was my job as the seller to in some way guide the person to understanding the need for my product.

Once I "got it" that people buy what they need in the way they need it, my beliefs about what constitutes sales changed and my behaviors had to change with it. The new behavior was spearheaded by my belief that I was stupid, that I didn't know what I was doing, and that the best I could do was get out of my own way.

I would never have discovered this new approach if I had been able to use my usual sales techniques.

Chapter 2

Bringing Your Values to Work

I'd like to continue my journey with you for a bit, because it didn't stop there. I had stumbled on a new selling approach and became very much the successful saleswoman: confident, in control, and a bit filled with my own importance.

I was so successful that I actually "retired" and moved back to the United States, to Taos, New Mexico, a place so individualistic, so laid back, so rural, so different from the rest of the country that when locals travel outside the state we're said to be "Going to America."

I must admit I was quite proud of myself when I arrived. I walked around the small town with the locals and believed I was better than they: I had money, I was successful, I was a world traveler. These people appeared poor and unsophisticated, living with few luxuries. I even let it be known that I was "better" than they were. My money, my Mercedes, my European acclaim, my real estate, were all topics of conversation. Of course I was ever so careful, in conversation, to make sure my "success" was discussed "tactfully," in light of the "difference" in our positions.

I had arrived in Taos during the Christmas holidays, so was originally happily swamped with parties. Within a few weeks, however, I noticed people I'd met weren't speaking to me when I'd see them on the street. "Hi!" I'd say brightly, and watch while people walked by as if we'd never met.

Oh well, there were other people I could be friends with . . . but there weren't. With a population of four thousand people, I kept running into the same people again and again. And they still didn't speak to me.

I had left behind my home, my friends, my now-former husband, my business. I was in a strange town with no friends, no work, and nothing to do. I filled up my time with hiking and walking and collecting stray dogs. I didn't know quite what to do with myself, since I'd worked nonstop for thirty years.

To fill my very free time and relieve my loneliness, I began getting involved with Native American ceremony: Native Americans were the only people who were willing to talk to me, and they seemed interesting, so I made a few new acquaintances.

Another Accident

One day, on a trip down to Santa Fe, I was in a major car accident. The driver of a fully loaded eighteen-wheeler found my stopped car in the way of his running a red light. My car was wrecked and my neck, back, and hip severely traumatized. I couldn't sit or walk and was in great pain.

My Native American friends came and got me after I had been home for a few weeks. They took me to a ceremony and sat up all night praying for me. In the morning, I walked—with a stick, but on my feet.

What had happened? I barely knew these people, but they were willing to do their healing magic for me.

I asked one of them why.

"When you are hurt, we are all hurt. We are one, all the same. We must help each other. Otherwise we're alone. And we weren't put here to be alone. The Creator has a plan for each of us, and we must help each other discover our own answers and heal as best we can, so each of us can use our unique gift to do the work the Creator wants us to do."

Another shock to my system. I realized that all my life I had worked from the assumption that I had to control my life and everything in it or nothing would happen, that it was me versus everyone else. I had pushed upstream for forty-three years and was constantly stressed, dealing with the issues I'd created and blamed on others, regularly involved with arguments and others' errors. Although I'd made a lot of money, I realized that the successful selling process I had discovered in my business happened by accident. And who was this Creator anyway?

If I chose to believe my friend, that a Creator was intervening, then maybe the way I discovered to sell was the unique gift she spoke of. I couldn't think of anything else I did that was truly unique. And if I were to be honest, on my own, I wouldn't have chosen a new way to sell given I had been happy with my old approach.

If truth be told, I had never been genuinely successful until I learned the new sales approach. I also realized that it wasn't just that I'd sold in a new way: I actually had managed my staff using the same communication principles, and taught them to work with clients the same way when they were in the field. Maybe there was something to that. Maybe that was my unique gift.

I had lots to think about. And I had lots of time to think.

I began reading—all the books I'd promised myself I'd read, and all the self-help books I could get my hands on. I had never done that before, since I didn't believe I fit into the same categories as anyone else, being so "special."

I began to realize that maybe I wasn't so special. Maybe I was just the same as everyone else. And maybe that was just fine. I continued to be involved with Native American ceremony doing drummings and dancing and sweat lodges. I began to get an understanding of this Creator, and how I was just a part of a bigger picture, small yet unique.

Mysteriously, people began talking to me again. People who had ignored me began inviting me to lunch. At first I was so hurt that I proudly turned away. But they persisted. I slowly accepted. I realized I needed them: they were my neighbors, my country-western dance partners, my car mechanics. I worked out with them, hiked with them, and sat next to them on the chairlift. They helped me push my car when it was stuck in the snow, and carried my dog home when she was hit by a car. I now had a home town. And it warmly welcomed me. I began to have a life filled with people and activity and time to read.

As my retirement moved into its second year, I began dreaming of a book. In my dreams I actually saw pages with words I could read. On these pages, all the values I had recently learned became enmeshed with my career. At first, the two seemed so disparate. Then I realized that what I had created in my sales technique in London was the embodiment of what I had learned my first months in Taos: we are all interdependent; we are here to serve each other; people come first; we all hold our own answers, answers that are unique to us but seem to fit into a more universal scheme.

Do Sales and Spirit Mix?

I wrote my first book, *Sales on the Line,* couching all my spiritual beliefs in sales terms. I thought no one would buy a sales book based on my spiritual values. I used the language of sales, telling curious friends, who knew my amalgamation of spiritual beliefs with sales methodology, that if you wanted to create a jailbreak, you had to hide the key in the loaf of bread, thereby creating freedom through nourishment. You certainly didn't give the jailer the extra key to hand to the prisoners. I was afraid that if I actually told salespeople I was putting spirituality into sales, they wouldn't buy the book or learn the new approach.

After all, salespeople were different. We were aggressive, demanding, quick, smart. A breed unto ourselves. More successful. Richer. Furiously independent. Had more self-esteem. And were definitely in control of our lives and livelihoods. How could

I discuss a way to think about sales that included giving up the type of control we were used to—the control that was so deeply rooted in the job description itself?

So I wrote a sales book that imbedded the values into the approach, without ever naming the values.

Business began to come in as a result of the book and I ended my retirement. The methodology worked. Sellers exceeded their targets. Companies made more revenue. Staff were happier. And clients discovered efficiently and effectively their own problems, solutions, and courses of action.

While I trained sellers in corporate America, I still didn't tell people what I was really doing. I just claimed it was a new sales methodology. But many course participants knew I was training more than sales.

"This is kind of . . . spiritual . . . isn't it? Like the Koran?" (Or Upanishads, or Bible, or whatever their persuasion might be.)

"Yes," I'd shyly admit. "But don't tell anyone else." I was scared to "come out."

Eventually, so many people would corner me with their secret understanding that I began telling selected clients that I was putting my spiritual principles into sales. Most of them knew. Others got curious. Some didn't care since the bottom-line results were so impressive.

None stopped working with me as a result.

During those early days of training sellers, I watched while the business world began to consider accepting spiritual values, calling the process "Spirituality at Work" and creating new models to encompass these values. I stayed stubborn, stating that sales was different, that salespeople would never buy this stuff.

When I began to write this book, I noticed how much effort I was using to couch the terms once again. I was twisting the spiritual values into an approach that sellers could learn as strictly a sales technique. After much inner turmoil, I decided to come out with my spiritual beliefs as the basis for the new sales approach.

Yet now, after training sellers in corporate America for three years, and after receiving hundreds of letters from sellers and readers of *Sales on the Line* thanking me for giving them permission to bring their hearts to work, I know salespeople, too, have been in turmoil. They have been leaving their hearts at home each day in order to go to work and sell.

So, as the decade moves into the new millennium, and some businesses are painstakingly working toward aligning their values, ethics, and principles with a greater good, I'm ready to champion the possibility of doing the same thing in sales. Without the sale of products and services, there can be no business. Therefore sales, as the building block upon which business rests, must incorporate these new ethical standards. Then businesses overall will have an easier time with change.

The Emerging Business Ethics

I have broadly defined the new business paradigm as: the inclusion of ethics, values, and principles in individual, company, and business dealings for the purpose of serving a greater good. As a result of this new paradigm, companies are beginning to consider structuring themselves by taking into account values such as the following:

Interdependence: through virtual companies and teams.

Creativity: through new production methods and increased expectations for input and output from individual workers.

Respect: through organization based on self-management and nonhierarchical reporting.

Community: by viewing teams and companies as families and through peer supervision.

Diversity: by allowing for and discovering excellence through multiple viewpoints and a wide range of skills.

Business can now become a daily exercise in helping to heal the world and each person in it. As Tom Chappell says in *The Soul of a Business:*

But if our souls aren't on the journey, if our quest is only about figuring our economic worth, it will be just another strategy, just another plan, just another game. Living and working are too important to let that happen. (p. 57)

Let's look at some of these shifts being considered in business and see how they relate to a new sales methodology.

Empowerment. Past iterations of sales approaches have given the seller *power over* the buyer. It's been win-lose. The new sales methodology empowers the buyer to make the best decision available, *whether or not the seller's product is the answer.* A relationship of trust and collaboration ensues; and the buyer gets exactly what she needs.

Quality. The Quality Movement is a management approach that ensures the highest standards and aims for complete customer satisfaction. The Quality Movement, however, has not fully addressed communication. But there is no other way to meet standards than by first finding out from the customer specifically what is needed and the way in which the customer wishes her needs met.

Service. Until now, sales has created an adversarial relationship in which one person has the answers that the other must defend herself against. In the true spirit of service, the new methodology has the seller serving the buyer by supporting the buyer in discovering how best to get her own needs met.

Partnership. In the nineties, there has been a recognition of the value of working with people and teams outside of our traditional areas of expertise. Virtual teams and companies have sprung up to supply value-added solutions where none existed before. The new sales methodology partners the seller and the buyer into a virtual team, with the seller taking responsibility for creating the structure of the team dynamic, and the buyer taking responsibility for providing the content around which the interaction takes place. Imagine a seller/buyer relationship in which there is immediate trust and belief that the best solution will emerge because they are working together to discover a solution.

Dialogue. In the art of dialoguing, groups sit together to discover a solution by trusting that one will arise out of the chaos of confusion. Each person offers her truth, with no expectation of a specific response. There is a basic trust that the best solution will come from the interplay among the participants.

Sales has not been at the forefront of this new business paradigm, this spiritual awakening. I suspect it is because

- until now, no sales methodology supported both spiritual values and making money;

- the current way of putting task first, instead of relationship, focuses on bottom-line numbers and has been more trackable;

- task orientation (a more masculine quality) has been more comfortable for the historic preponderance of male sellers, and the more feminine qualities of relationship and communication have not been stated as highly valued skills in business until now.

Melding the Masculine and the Feminine

One of the obvious characteristics of the emerging spiritually based business paradigm is the addition of feminine qualities. Because business has mainly been a male-based enterprise, the masculine qualities of left-brain, rational, task-based thinking have been predominant. But we've been out of balance. The emerging business paradigm has been incorporating the feminine qualities of relationship, creativity, trust, collaboration, and intuition.

Sales, as a task-based enterprise, has embodied masculine qualities. With emerging business paradigms based on principles and values, the feminine qualities of relationship and communication must be added into the equation for a balanced stance. In fact, we must begin to work toward a balance of the two.

According to Richard Tarnas in *The Passion of the Western Mind*:

This masculine dominance in Western intellectual history has certainly not occurred because women are any less intelligent than men. But can it be attributed *solely* to social restriction? I think not. I believe something more profound is going on here: something archetypical. The masculinity of the Western mind has been pervasive and fundamental, in both men and women, affecting every aspect of Western thought, determining its most basic conception of the human being and the human role in the world. (p. 441)

This is the great challenge of our time, the evolutionary imperative for the masculine to see through and overcome its hubris and one-sidedness, to own its unconscious shadow, to choose to enter into a fundamentally new relationship of mutuality with the feminine in all its forms. The feminine then becomes not that which must be controlled, denied, and exploited, but rather fully acknowledged, respected, and responded to for itself . . . [leading to a] profound and many-leveled marriage of the masculine and feminine . . . [whose synthesis] leads to something beyond itself: It brings an unexpected opening to a larger reality that cannot be grasped before it arrives. (pp. 444, 445)

To change our way of thinking about sales, to understand and sell within the ethics of the emerging new business paradigm and the integration of the masculine and feminine, we must first take on a new belief about what sales, and our role as sellers, entails.

The Values We Bring to Our Sales Jobs

Before you read further, I'd like you to take a few moments and answer the following questions as best you can.

- Is there a difference between the values you espouse in your personal life and those you espouse in your sales job? If so, what's the difference?

■ If there is a discrepancy in values, how does it show up: in your behavior? your attitude about work? your job satisfaction? your ability to make money?

■ To be congruent, what values would you put into your sales job? What's stopping you?

■ To be as effective and successful as you'd like to be as a salesperson and maintain your personal values, what behaviors would you need to keep? to change? What would stop you?

■ Do you believe that it's possible to have ethical, spiritually based values while in the profession of sales? What skills would you need to support that possibility? What behaviors would be different? How would your job be different? What benefits would you gain? What losses would you incur?

My job, both as seller and author, is to support your process of discovery. Through this book, I offer you the opportunity to develop congruence between the principles you live by in your daily life and those necessary to be a successful seller. They needn't be disparate. In fact, you can be more successful as a seller by taking your spiritual values to work.

The question becomes: what skills and behaviors do you use to embody your values while getting your products and services sold? The new sales approach that I'm offering in this book addresses this question by including the beliefs that every person

■ holds her own answers;

■ is capable of making valid decisions in the most practical time frame;

■ wants to be in honest, trustworthy relationships;

■ wishes her uniqueness to be honored and respected;

■ prefers to do her job to the best of her capabilities.

In the business of sales, we must rethink our very definition of what sales is, in order to work with these beliefs.

Ethics and the Bottom Line:

Can We Do Well and Do Good at the Same Time?

I often hear sales managers and company presidents say that they fear that working with new business paradigm thinking will not translate to the bottom line, or that it won't be definable as cost effective. Working from personal spiritual values and the new business paradigm does not preclude making money. It just means you'll make money congruently and consistently with your values, and support individual, group, company, and global change. And because it is sales, you will be able to monitor and track effectiveness easily.

In alignment with my stated spiritual values, which are used as the foundation of my sales approach, I am devoting this book to giving you

- the skills to incorporate new paradigm thinking and your spiritual values into your selling approach;

- the principles, skills, applications, and beliefs inherent in this new sales technology;

- assistance in discovering how to be as effective a sales professional as you can be while remaining congruent with your personal beliefs and ethics;

- a sales methodology that will bring in substantially more revenue while enhancing the thinking process of your prospects and clients.

I trust that you have your own answers. My job is to ask the questions that will assist you in discovering how to be the most effective salesperson you wish to be, with increased financial reward if you wish it, while acting on your personal ethical principles.

SKILL SET #1:

Bringing Your Values to Work

☐ What values do you believe in and use when communicating with another person? Please spend some time delineating them.

☐ What values do you believe in and use when communicating with a prospective buyer? When selling? Are these values different from those you believe in and use during other communications?

☐ What communication behaviors do you use when you sell effectively? ineffectively? And what is the difference? Do these communication behaviors support your values?

☐ Do you use different rapport-building skills for friends, family, and prospective buyers? If so, what are the differences? Why are there differences? Are your values a part of the way you communicate? If so, what are the differences in the way they are applied in each instance?

☐ What skills do you use to close a sale? to gather information? What is the difference in the skills you use when you are effective versus the skills you use when you are ineffective? Do you communicate by using your values in either instance?

☐ What would you do differently if you were selling effectively all the time? What's stopping you from being effective consistently? Would using your personal values make a difference in how effective you are? What would be the difference?

☐ What would have to be different for you to bring your personal values into your sales job?

Chapter 3

The Principles of Buying Facilitation

I am using the term Buying Facilitation to describe the new relationship-based, solution-focused, and ethically oriented sales approach. Buying Facilitation serves a different function than selling. I define it as

a questioning and listening process, for the purpose of serving, that facilitates a buyer's discovery of how best to get his or her needs met.

Selling has been focused on how sellers sell rather than on how buyers buy, with the intent to move product as the sole reason for buyer-seller affiliation. Of course, as sellers, your job description does not include gratuitously seeking out strangers to facilitate their discovery about any unsolved problems they have. But you can use the Buying Facilitation process as a way to both further your own development as a service provider and support your prospect's development—on the same dime. Win-win.

There are six principles that I believe embody both ethics and sales. I've discovered that when I work with these principles, I can support prospects in discovering how, what, when, and if they need a new solution, and whether my product fits their need, in a fraction of the time it took using the old way. While they appear simple, the principles deviate greatly from the way sellers have historically been taught to think about selling.

The Six Principles

1. *You have nothing to sell if there's no one to buy.*

2. *Relationship comes first, task second.*

3. *The buyer has the answers; the seller has the questions.*

4. *Service is the goal; discovery is the outcome; a sale may be the solution.*

5. *People buy only when they can't fill their own needs.*

6. *People buy using their own buying patterns, not a seller's selling patterns.*

Let's take a closer look at each one of the principles.

1. You have nothing to sell if there's no one to buy.

Sales used to be an activity to move product. But when a seller seeks to place a product by searching for someone who will buy, it's a solution in search of a problem.

The simple truth is, you can't make a sale without a buyer. And contrary to what most sales approaches teach, it's the buyer who has the answers, who understands the complexity of the issues. If a prospect does not discover what he needs to buy, when he needs to buy it, how he needs to buy it, and how to integrate a solution into his team or group or family, it doesn't matter what your product is or how well you sell it.

The sales process as we've known it disrespects a buyer's ability to solve his own problems. This basic, inherent effrontery has created an inability for the seller to establish a trusting interaction with the prospect. When sellers assume they have the answer and the prospect doesn't, it's automatically one-up, one-down. How could a prospect possibly trust a seller?

Recently I was interviewing and speaking with the president of a Fortune 500 entertainment company. He had called every reference I gave him, been given letters of referral, met with me in different cities, and was delightful and friendly each time we spoke. But he wasn't able to decide what he wanted in the way of sales training. He didn't seem to be interviewing with any other training companies, so I was confused.

I finally called him to ask what was going on, stating that I must have missed something in my questions or he would have known what he wanted for sales training.

"There's a problem I have avoided discussing. We have a chief operations officer (COO) who makes Hitler look like a teddy bear. If I don't have all the numbers for him and the ducks in a row, he won't come up with the check. He has no right brain, and all my belief about your work, all my intuition, is meaningless. "

Once I was offered more complete information about what the issues were—and I was more fully trusted as a result of the purpose of my call—I was invited to offer concrete recommendations about how to support the COO's style in terms of making a buying decision.

While it initially seemed like a simple decision to me, the buyer had obstacles to work out prior to making a decision to buy. Without being a company employee, I could not fully comprehend them.

Your job is to help a prospect with a problem discover how to get from here to there in your product's area of expertise. It may be that you can help him discover how to best use his internal resources, how to find another more appropriate product, or, as in the example above, assist in the company's decision-making process. If you "make a sale," it's because it is the best solution. But the sale becomes the by-product of the interaction—not the goal.

2. Relationship comes first, task second.

Your ultimate goal as a seller is to serve. You must learn to flip the focus and put *relationship* before *task*, *being* before *doing*. Sure, you must understand the tasks, who is involved in the buying process, and how much is in the budget. Yes, sometimes analyzing your prospect base gives you answers. *But unless you find a buyer who wants to work with you, there is no need for your product, so putting task first sets you up for failure.* All the marketing and production, all the packaging and analysis, all the great pitches are for nothing if a buyer doesn't want to buy the product. And you can't sell a product unless there is a level of comfort and trust between you and your prospect. *People only buy from people they like.* Dale Carnegie taught us that sixty years ago. He just taught the behaviors around making people like you as a *task* without addressing the beliefs or skills that make *relationship* possible.

An extreme example of this is those telemarketing calls that always seem to come at night, just when we're tired or busy. The telemarketers are clear as to what we should buy, and they'll tell us by pitch, by script, or just by persistence. The part that is so annoying is being treated like a number, just the next person on their automatic dialer. We might even need the product, but because the seller is playing a numbers game and we are just a number—a task instead of a person—we are turned off.

We'd like to think that as sales professionals we are doing it differently. But though we may be treated with more respect than most telemarketers, I believe we are essentially doing the same thing with our prospects.

I sat in a coaching session with a seller while he tried to get through to a company manager he'd been trying to reach for weeks. He placed the call and was greeted by a woman. He began the call by speaking in a very officious, commanding voice.

"Hi. I'd like to speak with Shelly, please. Is she in?"

"Sorry, she's on vacation and won't be back for two weeks. Want to leave a message?"

"No, thanks, I'll call back."

After he hung up I asked him to place the call again so I could try it. The salesman was surprised.

"But she's on vacation."

To humor me, he dialed the number and handed me the phone.

"Hello. This is Sharon Drew Morgen. Who am I speaking with, please?"

"Kathleen."

"Hi. This is a sales call, and I'm wondering if this is a good time to speak. I'm with SCS Corp."

"From SCS? I've been trying to get help from you guys for two months. I have a broken printer of yours here, and no one in your company will help me get it fixed! I'm furious!"

"That's terrible! I'm so sorry. How awful to buy an expensive piece of equipment and not be able to get proper service."

"I'm so mad I've just taken you out of my budget for next year. I wouldn't buy anything from you ever again."

"I don't blame you. What would you like me to do first to start the process to get the machine repaired?"

"Hang on, let me get my area manager, Shelly, on the line so the three of us can have a conference call and discuss this."

The salesman was quite surprised. He couldn't understand why he'd been told the woman was on vacation when she was in fact in the office.

He had forgotten to get into relationship with the woman who answered the phone. He was doing the job of calling on a customer, and since the woman who answered wasn't Shelly—i.e., not his customer—he didn't bother to get into relationship with her. She responded by not getting into relationship with him, either. Lose-lose. No one likes to be treated like a task, a thing. Put relationship first. Without people in our business equation, we don't have any tasks to do anyway.

3. The buyer has the answers; the seller has the questions.

Until now, sellers have approached a prospect from the standpoint of having "the answer." For me, this assumption makes sales a win-lose proposition: "My product is the answer, so either I'll tell you why (Traditional sales) or we can discover together (Consultative sales) how you can best use it." Assuming you have another person's answer is disrespectful, condescending, and patronizing. It does not support empowerment, collaboration, service, quality, or partnership.

If the seller has the answers, the buyer is left with the questions. And what questions do buyers ask themselves? Questions about the seller! Initially they have no other questions to ask, since they often don't know which questions to ask themselves. That's where your expertise comes in. *When you assume your buyer has the answers, it becomes your job to create the questions that will allow him to find those answers.*

And you know your buyer has the answers because each one of you, as independent thinkers, as adults who have thrived, grown, made mistakes, and generally survived in this game of life, have had to create a way to make sense of a world uniquely your own. It is difficult, if not impossible, for another person to have your answers for you, even if you might need to seek outside help from time to time. As a seller you have made a career out of knowing what's right for other people. When using Buying Facilitation, you trust that another has his own answers; you are actually empowering him to reach his potential.

Let me give you a simple analogy of what it's like when people assume they have our answers. Imagine what it would be like if you went into a Chinese restaurant and the waiter came over with his order book.

"So, you'll have spareribs and chow mein."

"No. Hello. I'd like to see a menu, please. I'm not sure what I want."

"You don't need a menu. I know what you want. It's our special tonight. It's priced fairly and it's delicious. It'll be spareribs and chow mein. Believe me, I can tell that's what you'd like."

You wouldn't let a waiter do that. But as sellers you do it all the time: I know what you need, and what you need is my product.

4. *Service is the goal; discovery is the outcome; a sale may be the solution.*

When you enter into a selling interaction with the purpose of making a sale, you are predetermining an outcome. The prospect ends up defending himself. When you enter into a selling interaction with the purpose of serving, the prospect feels he is being supported in his decision and will trust the seller enough to begin a collaboration.

I recently looked into hiring a well-thought-of man to be my media coach. He sent me his marketing materials. In a beautiful, expensively produced booklet, there were thirty-two pages of references and testimonials, and five pages that told me what the company did, how successful they were, and how many important contacts they had. When the man phoned me to follow up, I told him I didn't think we could work together because I didn't see any room for me to work "with" him, as a partnership. He became so very sweet. Didn't I understand that he was an expert and that he'd know exactly what I needed and that he could make me successful?

"But what about my expertise and my needs to form a collaboration?" I asked.

"If you're my client, then we don't have to collaborate. I'll take care of everything."

"It sounds like you're patronizing me."

"Not at all. In fact I resent your saying that. I treat everyone as an equal. I'm just doing my job."

"What about serving me? I didn't notice anything in your marketing materials that would lead me to believe you'd want to find my specific needs—which are values-based."

"My marketing materials were created to sell. Once I sell, then I serve. People want to know they're getting an expert, and my materials were created to convince them that I'm the best. People decide to hire me when they see how many other important people have chosen to work with me."

"Well, you lost me. I would have wanted to work with you if you had called me and asked me what my needs were and what I needed in order to form a collaboration with you. For me, it's service first, then I'll buy. I don't think your values are close enough to mine for us to work together."

"It has nothing to do with values. People hire me because I'm an expert. I know my business and I'm good."

"But it doesn't matter to me how good you are if I can't work with you in the way that's comfortable for me."

Why is it assumed that selling and convincing are part of the same sentence? Where are our values in all this? Tied up in our product? In our sales approach? In the product's production? In our closing ratio? In our commission checks? *Why has it been okay all these years to circumvent our values and perpetuate a profession that bases its monetary compensation on disrespecting people?*

Throughout modern sales history as we know it, no approach has given the seller the job of serving the prospect and supporting him in discovering how best to get his needs met—separate from selling the seller's product.

With your goal as service, and the outcome the prospect's discovery of how best to get his needs met, you become the servant to the prospect, part of the team, and in service to the common good. The solution may be a sale. It may be the prospect's ability to use internal resources more effectively. It may even be a competitor's product. In any case, you will have served this person, and quickly. You will both know, in one, possibly two contacts, what the outcome of the connection will be.

5. *People buy only when they can't fill their own needs.*

Previous sales approaches have missed the point: *there is no way that you, as a seller who is outside the company culture, outside the decision-making body, can really know what is going on with your new prospects.* You might even become part of the team, a well-respected collaborator. But you remain external to the process.

Prospects must experience substantial motivation to search for external resources to solve a problem, given the amount of disruption it incurs. Not only is there cultural and political disruption, there may also be ego issues.

People are hired within companies to fix things. They keep on getting paid only when they have shown some level of success. No matter how fixable a problem, if an outside resource is needed (unless sought to address organizational change), the implication is that someone, somehow, might have been unsuccessful. That means they have to believe they might be even more unsuccessful if they don't do something different from what they've already done.

Primarily, a person seeking resources outside their company must be completely comfortable knowing that whatever they've got in place will not answer their needs.

When you take a good look at the elements that must be examined prior to a buying decision, you can see how sales until now has created distrust between buyer and seller. Sales has been about selling product, not supporting the buying process. It actually has distrusted the buyer's ability to make appropriate choices in his unique environment, focusing instead on the seller having the answers.

6. People buy using their own buying patterns, not a seller's selling patterns.

When you were taught to sell, you were taught to open, close, pitch, present, handle objections, and deal with rejection—all skills which in fact limit your audience of prospective buyers to those people who buy the way you sell. Everyone who needs the product but feels uncomfortable with your approach *will not buy,* regardless of whether or not they have a need.

I recently trained a group of salespeople from a Fortune 100 company who were selling hardware peripherals in a secondary market. The initial hardware had been purchased in a prior sale, and these second-tier salespeople were making follow-up calls to track the progress of the hardware and sell any additional items or upgrades the clients needed.

One young man sat quietly for two days during the sales training. On the day I was to spend one-on-one time with him, he greeted me with a grunt and a sigh of exasperation. I sat down. He looked away.

"You don't want me here, do you?"

"No, not really."

"You are one of the top producers and are doing just fine without me, right?"

"That's about it in a nutshell."

"So here's what we'll do. Since I've already been paid to sit with you, how about if I listen to one call, offer some suggestions, and have you do one more. Then if you want me to leave I will."

He sighed. He grudgingly picked up the phone, and I heard this conversation from his end.

"Hi. Is this Ms. Jones? This is John Smith from ABC Corp. Got a minute? . . . I'm your new rep, following up your purchase of the 123 machine you just got. How's it working for you? . . . Good,

good. I'm just calling to introduce myself and thought I'd leave you my name and number in case you need anything—like add-ons or additional software or something. Got a pen?"

After he put the phone down, he looked quite satisfied with himself.

"Is that how all of your introductory calls go? Would you be willing to try just one call in a new way? And then you could go back to your way afterwards? But since it's just one call, you'll really have to try to do it differently."

After I got agreement, I wrote down some questions for him to address. I had noticed his call had been dependent on his having the answers and on his confidence that he'd created enough rapport for Ms. Jones to call him back—lots of assumptions.

On the next call, he opened with my preferred opening and some of the questions I suggested to create a collaboration.

"Hi. My name is John Smith from ABC Corp. Who am I speaking with please? . . . Mr. Turner, you were the person I was going to ask for. This is a service call. Is this a good time for us to speak? . . . Could you tell me how your new system is running and how it is affecting your environment? . . . So it sounds like the system is fine and that your team is in learning mode right now . . . What would you need to do or have to support that learning curve? . . . It sounds like you have all the resources you need in-house. That's good. Is there anything you are missing that could help you get your environment working better? . . . It sounds like with the in-house training support available there you've got that handled in-house also. I'm also hearing that many of your people have been around a long time with other systems and are challenged with this new one. Do you have any new people coming in who know the system and who could help the other folks? . . . That's an awful lot of new people coming in. What type of arrangements have you made for them to work with the new system, since that number of users cannot work together on one system . . . Ah, I thought you knew that. What information do you need from me about users on the new system? . . . So now that you know that, what more do you need to be able to support your future environment? . . . The price of an add-on for that many users is $XX. Yeah, it's high. Do you have a budget for that right now? . . . Oh good. Since you are creating next year's budget this month I can get you numbers to put in so at least they will be there when and if it's time. What specifically do you need from me to help you in getting your budget right? . . . Sure, I can fax that over to you. Is there anything else you need from me? . . . How would you know that the supplementary hardware we're talking about will give you what you need? . . . Sure, I can send you the specs with the prices. Anything else?"

When the salesman got off the phone, he stared at the wall without a word. He blinked a few times, let out a huge sigh, and said, "Okay, I'll take my lumps like a man. That sale was just moved forward one year, since he wouldn't have figured out he needed that for six months and it wouldn't have been in his budget. He may not have even called *me* to place the order."

In the first scenario, there was a seller but no buyer. In the second scenario, there was collaboration, trust, and rapport. The seller was serving the buyer. And it was win-win.

When we support the buyer in making the best decision available *whether or not the seller's product is the answer,* a relationship of trust and collaboration ensues. And the seller will close more sales due to finding the right people sooner.

SKILL SET #2:

The Principles

Think about the principles you have been working from in your sales approach. Ask yourself the following questions:

- [ ] How do you think a sale occurs? What part do you currently play in making it happen?

- [ ] What is your goal as you enter the dialogue with your prospect or buyer? How rigidly do you carry that goal as the call progresses? What behaviors do you present in order to maintain your purpose? Have your behaviors ever gotten in the way of a sale? Or do you change your behavior as necessary?

☐ If you change your behavior to be in alignment with your prospective buyer, does your goal change?

☐ Assume that your goal is service and not to sell your product. How would you approach the sales call? What would be different in your approach?

☐ What would you do differently if you put relationship before task? What behaviors would you use? not use?

☐ If you realize your product is inappropriate for the prospect, what do you do?

☐ What specifically are your selling patterns? Delineate the behaviors you use to "do" your selling patterns.

Chapter 4

Comparing the Past, Present, and Future of Sales

Buying Facilitation believes it's the seller's job to facilitate discovery to support a buyer who has her own answers. This is such a different belief and requires such different skills that I'll compare previous sales methodologies to Buying Facilitation in this chapter to aid your understanding before going more deeply into the skills. Historically, the goal of the seller has been to sell product using strategies to influence or convince buyers in the most effective way possible. As I see it, the new goal of the seller is to support a buyer's ability to solve her own problems with existent resources where possible, or external resources where necessary.

The Buying Facilitation Process

Let me begin by leading you through a brief example of the Buying Facilitation process to give you an idea of what I'm talking about and what to consider while comparing the traditional and consultative methodologies with Buying Facilitation. I take a risk here since much of what you will notice me doing goes against what has been taught traditionally. But given Buying Facilitation's new belief structure, new behaviors are in order.

While you are not yet familiar with the specific elements unique to Buying Facilitation contained within the example, there are a few elements I'd like you to be aware of up front. Notice the role the facilitator (seller) plays to guide and support the buyer by creating a structure for the call enabling them to move quickly through issues that can take several contacts in more traditional approaches. Also notice how little the product content is mentioned. *The focus of the call is the prospect's discovery of what she needs rather than her understanding of what the seller is selling.*

At the end of the example, I'll ask you some questions to help you see the differences between the way you sell and the Buying Facilitation method.

I'll start with a phone contact as most sales begin there.

"Hello. This is Gina Manor."

"Hello. This is Sharon Drew Morgen with XBA Office Supplies. This is a sales call. Is this a good time to speak?"

GM: "A sales call? What are you selling?"

SDM: "I guess it depends on what you need to buy. Is this a good time? You sound like it is."

GM: "Sure. Shoot."

SDM: "Could you tell me what you're doing around purchasing office supplies?"

GM: "Yeah. We read the catalogues that come out every week and put in orders for the sale items."

SDM: "That sounds like a plan. Does it get all your supply needs covered?"

GM: "Pretty much. Of course, sometimes we find we run out when an item hasn't been advertised for a while, but generally it works."

SDM: "Has there ever been a time when you used one supplier?"

GM: "Briefly. I would place an order weekly and would sometimes see an item advertised cheaper in one of the catalogues. And sometimes I would forget something and have to do an emergency order, which they were not always able to get to me when I needed it. What I'm doing now seems to work just as well as that did, and I think it saves us a little money."

SDM: "I see that money is a highly valued criterion of yours."

GM: "You bet. Isn't it for everyone?"

SDM: "Money is one of those important commodities. Is it your only criterion for deciding how to manage your supplies?"

GM: "No. I also need to have appropriate supplies for the employees, and make sure I have quality merchandise. If I can get all my needs met and get great prices, I'm a happy camper. I'm much more concerned about having the right supplies available for the company."

SDM: "So I hear price is important but timing and quality are also important. I'm assuming you are getting all three criteria met now."

GM: "Mostly. Sometimes, when I forget to order something, I can't always get the item in my time frame. Then I have to run around to find it, and usually have to pay top dollar for it. I'm afraid that part is the downside of doing it myself. But nothing is perfect."

SDM: "Could you tell me if there are any conditions under which you would consider using one supplier again?"

GM: "I don't think there are. Well, maybe. I guess the only way would be if I could be assured I was getting the best prices, and I got delivery when I needed it, and maybe some type of an emergency delivery service. If I couldn't get it done better than I'm doing it now, why bother?"

SDM: "So I hear you saying you are happy with the way you are doing things, that you get the best prices, and that you would only consider changing if you could be assured that you'd at least get the service and prices you are already getting. Is that right?"

GM: "It is. What have you got?"

SDM: "I'll tell you after another few questions, if you don't mind. Could you tell me about the time it takes you to keep your system going? I'm asking because one of our services is to come into your supply area and see what you need, and I noticed you are doing that part yourself."

GM: "You mean, you'd come in and take stock for me?"

SDM: "That's one of our services. You may or may not need it, depending on your time factor."

GM: "I never thought of that. I guess I just thought that was part of the job. I guess I'd save about four hours a week if someone else did that for me. Do you charge for that?"

SDM: "No, that's part of the service. But if you've factored that in to your normal work week, and it's working for you, you may not be interested in that aspect of our service."

GM: "I never knew I had an option. How about your prices? Do you have a catalogue? Weekly specials? How do you compare with the other suppliers?"

SDM: "I'm hearing you are interested in what we're doing here, but I'd really like to know how you'd know when it was time to bring in an outside group? What you're doing has worked well for you. I could have the best product in the world, and if what you are doing works for you, you don't need me."

GM: "You made me think about saving time. If I could save time, and get fair prices, and have all the supplies I need when I need them, I'd consider using a supplier. What company did you say you were with again?"

SDM: "XBA Office Supplies. How would you know that my company could provide all those things for you?"

GM: "Do you have references in my line of business? Could you send me their names? Maybe you could send one of your catalogues. And some information on that supply service. Could you get me that information?"

SDM: "Sure. But what would you be looking for in the references and in the materials? How would you know that what we have would serve you? And is there anyone else in your company that you'd want to bring into the loop so we could all meet and discuss your needs?"

GM: "Good point. Sometimes the chief financial officer (CFO) gets involved, since we purchase a high volume of supplies. I could have a talk with her and give you her number, if I like your materials. I'd want to see if your prices are similar to the other suppliers. And I'd want to find out from the referrals if you are timely and responsible—if you stand behind your products."

SDM: "You know, we can't always keep up with all the competition. Since money is such a highly valued criterion of yours, how would you want to deal with the fact that you might occasionally see an item cheaper?"

GM: "If your prices are consistently fair, I'd understand that you can't always match the competition. But over time, I'd have to understand that I'd be coming out a winner."

SDM: "And how would you want us to stay on top of that?"

GM: "Could we have bimonthly discussions for the first few months? And would you be willing to in some way compensate me if I think something is not right?"

SDM: "That sounds okay to me. And I will be sure to send you several weeks worth of our catalogues so you can check and see how our prices stack up. Where do you want us to go from here?"

GM: "Send me all the information and referrals. In fact, if you can get it to me by Friday, you can speak with the CFO on Monday when she's in. I'll be waiting for your call Friday afternoon, if that's okay with you. If I'm not around, I'll leave the CFO's number with my secretary and will have spoken to her in the morning. If all looks as good as it sounds, I'd like to get started on the first of the month. Would that be okay with you?"

No Objections

When people first come in contact with the Buying Facilitation method, they are surprised that one call can get so far into the sales cycle so quickly. Notice that I didn't pitch or have an opening speech. I also accepted her decisions and remained in agreement with her throughout, letting her know I respected what she was doing, which I did. As a result, there were no objections, since the prospective buyer was supported in her current decisions and in getting her own needs met: I trusted that her answers worked for her.

She discovered what worked, what didn't, what she would

need for change, and how she would potentially want to work with me. When I asked her, "Are there any conditions under which you would consider using one supplier again?" she could just as easily have decided that there were none. If that happened, I would have asked for a referral and ended the call. Anything else would have disrespected her right to make the choices she believed served her company the best.

This is a simplistic example to give you an understanding of the way Buying Facilitation works. I will be offering more complex examples and issues as we progress. Take a moment now, though, and note the differences between this interaction and one you might have had given the same sales situation. This exercise will begin to highlight your current beliefs, skills, and behaviors as sellers to give you a clearer idea of the differences in approaches.

- How would you have opened the call? Would you have introduced yourself differently? Mentioned your product sooner or in more detail? Generally operated differently, given it was a cold call?

- What types of questions would you have asked? If they are different from the ones I asked, how are they different and what would be the difference in results?

- Would the call have taken a different direction from mine? How? Would that have changed the outcome? If so, how?

- How would you have ended/closed the call?

Comparing the Old and the New

Before introducing the basic beliefs of Buying Facilitation, I'd like to analyze the beliefs we've assumed over the last sixty or so years, which we have incorporated into our daily selling behaviors. Once you understand what you've thought of as sales until now, you'll be able to more clearly recognize the differences Buying Facilitation offers. As an editor of a magazine said recently, after finding it difficult to grasp this new sales concept, "I see a seller's job as finding the best way possible to let prospects know what her product is and how it fits in with their needs." And so it has been.

On the next page is a chart that compares the elements of Traditional and Consultative selling approaches to the elements of Buying Facilitation so that you can see the differences clearly. This will help you to understand how differences in beliefs create different behaviors, and how these behaviors have kept you from being as effective as you might want to be. It is interesting to note that while you may think you've come so far from the Traditional sales approach, in reality you have incorporated much of that tradition into your common beliefs about sales today.

Traditional Sales: The Beliefs

In Traditional methodologies—Carnegie, Zigler, Professional Selling Skills (Xerox), to name the most obvious ones—sales is

Seller-Based

Product-Focused

Task-Based

It looks like this:

Buyer ⟵——— *Seller* ———⟶ *Product*

The main beliefs are:

1. *The seller has the control and power in the interaction.*
   Traditional sales made a point of this: if the buyer didn't buy it was because the seller didn't do a good enough job of selling. Know your product! Know your customer! Have a great opening! Know how to handle objections! Work on that pitch! Lead the prospect where you want her! This belief goes hand in hand with

2. *It's the seller's job to convince the prospect to buy the product.*
   Although many words were used—persuade, influence, manipulate, sway, win over—it came down to this.

Comparing Traditional and Consultative Sales with Buying Facilitation

Traditional Sales: The Beliefs

1. The seller has the control and power in the interaction.

2. It's the seller's job to convince the prospect to buy the product.

3. Everyone needs the product. They just have to be made to understand that they need it.

4. People who don't buy are jerks.

5. It's a numbers game. Contact enough people and you'll make your numbers.

6. Buyers lie and cannot be trusted.

7. The seller has the answers and drives the sale.

8. Prospects don't know what they need.

The Skills

1. Product knowledge

2. Open, pitch, present, close

3. Controlling the interaction

4. Objection handling

Consultative Sales: The Beliefs

1. The seller has control over the ultimate outcome, but shares control with the buyer during the interaction.

2. It's the seller's job to make the appropriate information available in a collaborative setting.

3. The prospect will probably need the product once s/he recognizes what s/he is missing.

4. People who don't buy are making a big mistake.

5. It's still a numbers game.

6. Prospects are guarded and keep their cards close to their chest.

7. The seller has the answers but the prospect supplies critical input.

8. Prospects think they know what they need, but need help from sellers to get it right.

The Skills

1. Extensive product knowledge

2. Open, pitch, present, close

3. Questioning and listening skills

4. Presentation skills

5. Negotiation skills

Buying Facilitation: The Beliefs

1. The prospect has ultimate control over the outcome of the interaction.

2. The seller's job is to support the prospective buyer's needs.

3. The prospective buyer knows what s/he needs and can solve his/her own problems with the support of the seller's questions.

4. People buy only when they cannot solve their problem with their own internal resources; then they seek an external solution.

5. Sellers will find the right people to buy their product independent of their need to sell.

6. Prospective buyers and sellers trust each other and are honest with each other, communicating in a "We Space" uniquely their own.

7. Prospective buyers have the answers, sellers have the questions.

8. Prospective buyers know what they need but prefer to work collaboratively with a seller in a win-win situation to support each other in getting their needs met.

The Skills

1. Ability to move between communication choice points to ensure understanding and continued rapport

2. Questioning and listening skills

3. Responsibility for collaborative communication

4. Ability to shift communication skills to support the beliefs, needs, and culture of the buyer

5. Trust, rapport, and respect

3. *Everyone needs the product. They just have to be made to understand that they need it.*

This belief supports the previous beliefs. Since it's the seller's job to be in control, every prospect is a candidate to buy and if they don't, belief number four kicks in.

4. *People who don't buy are jerks.*

The favorite word of disgruntled sellers.

5. *It's a numbers game. Contact enough people and you'll make your numbers.*

Sellers have their chosen selling patterns. As long as they continue to sell using personal behavioral patterns, they will only sell to those people who buy the way they sell. Hence, lots of contacts.

6. *Buyers lie and cannot be trusted.*

Of course. Since the seller enters with her own agenda, she sets up an adversarial relationship. The natural consequence is for the buyer to be less than honest.

7. *The seller has the answers and drives the sale.*

After all that product training, the seller should know more than the buyer!

8. *Prospects don't know what they need.*

How can they? They are always saying "I don't know." Their conscious brain has no ready answers, so it's obvious they don't know.

Traditional Sales: The Skills

Let's look at the skills the seller needs to support these beliefs. I'm going to be a bit playful here, but I want to dramatize the underlying messages the buyer receives when faced with these approaches.

Product Knowledge

When you know all the ins and outs of your product you can wow buyers with the brilliance of your solution. Make sure you don't make a mistake—they won't buy from you if you get it wrong. . . . But they will if you get it right! Especially if you can run down the benefits.

Open, Pitch, Present, Close

These skills were developed during the Traditional sales era and are still being used in virtually all sales training. Notice how these skills are used to control the interaction, with the assumption that the product is the answer.

Controlling the Interaction

A definite skill set: learn the different personality types to know how to counter objections; give buyers only two choices so they'll have to say yes to one of them; grab them with a great opening; lure them into a friendly conversation as quickly as possible so they'll like you enough to buy from you; use their names often and ask them how they are so they will think you like them.

Objection Handling

Once you learn all the objections a buyer might throw at you, you'll know how to counter them and break the back of the objection. Too much money? Well, Ma'am, what is it costing you to not use our product? This isn't the right time? Well, Ma'am, isn't it the wrong time when you don't have the benefits our product will give you? How much are you losing by not buying it now? Or should I call you in two weeks and give you time to change your mind?

Here's a summary of how Traditional sales works.

A typical salesperson learns product information, learns the best ways to pitch the product, gets mailing lists or referrals, spends prospecting time finding people to sit with face-to-face, and through presentation and pitch, tells prospects why they need the seller's product. It is assumed there will be objections to overcome and lack of sophistication on the part of the buyer in terms of what she *really* needs. It is the seller's job to get the prospect to truly understand that the seller's product will fill unmet and not-understood needs.

As you can see, much of the skill set and belief patterns of the traditional sales approach remains with us today.

Consultative Sales: The Beliefs

Now let's look at the sales approaches of the late eighties and early nineties—those decades when spiritual values and ethics became spoken about and even accepted as a commercial adjunct to better business practices—and how much farther they take us to where we ultimately want to be.

There have been major changes in sales in the past ten years or so, starting with Larry Wilson's *Changing the Game* in 1987 and *SPIN Selling* by Neil Rackham in 1988. People and relationship have been added to the equation.

The Consultative approach has come a long way toward including the prospect in the interaction, toward attempting to make the prospect part of the process. It's the next stage in the continuum toward sales based on spiritual values. These approaches don't *tell* prospects what they need; they *ask* them questions (based on the seller's product being the answer) and *then* tell the prospects why they need the product. Yet the underlying basic structure remains the same as in Traditional sales, as we shall see.

If you are using a mixture of Consultative approaches, check if you have the belief that you have the answer and your product is it. If you are using any influencing strategies to promote your product, with a primary goal of making a sale, you are also, by definition, creating an adversarial relationship. *Objections are the natural result of buyers defending themselves against sellers who are trying to get their own needs met.*

In Consultative methodologies—SPIN Selling, Sandler Sales, High Probability Selling, Strategic Selling, Solution Selling—sales is

Seller- and Buyer-Based

Product-Focused

Task-Based

It looks like this:

Prospect ⟵⟶ Seller ⟶ Product

The main beliefs are:

1. ***The seller has control over the ultimate outcome, but shares control with the buyer during the interaction.***

   A relationship with the buyer is now important. This translates to mean a seller cannot do it alone and needs to ask the buyer to join in. It is even an important value that the customer get her needs met. Ultimately, however, the product is still the likely answer and the relationship between buyer and seller will serve to highlight the product as the solution.

2. ***It's the seller's job to make the appropriate information available in a collaborative setting.***

   Although buyer and seller are collaborating, the onus is on the seller to present the necessary information.

3. ***The prospect will probably need the product once she recognizes what she is missing.***

   The belief that the product is the answer prevails. After all, why sell if not to support your product?

4. ***People who don't buy are making a big mistake.***

   They're not jerks anymore—but they are wrong. Oh, some people probably don't need the product, but they could probably use it if they were really honest.

5. ***It's still a numbers game.***

   Smile and dial. Call enough people and you'll find buyers. Of course, there is some truth to this: when sellers continue to use their own selling patterns, they must seek those people that buy the way they sell.

6. ***Prospects are guarded and keep their cards close to their chest.***

   This relationship stuff is great, but if the seller believes the answer is the product, the prospect still doesn't trust that her interests are being served.

7. ***The seller has the answers but the prospect supplies critical input.***

   At least the buyer is being consulted!

8. *Prospects think they know what they need, but need help from sellers to get it right.*

Sellers pose some questions and listen for a while—and then come in with the answers. Sellers really think they have the answers still. But it's confusing, given their push to consult.

It's obvious and exciting that the foundation of sales has shifted. But the basic intention remains the same, with some accommodation for the prospective buyer's input.

Consultative Sales: The Skills

Here are the skills necessary to support the relationship-based sales methodology.

Extensive Product Knowledge

Since the prospect has so much input, the seller needs a great deal of preparation in order to have the necessary information and answers.

Open, Pitch, Present, Close

Still in use, but with the buyer's input.

Questioning and Listening Skills

Since a sale cannot proceed without input from the buyer, the seller needs to know how to ask the right questions. And to ask the right questions demands fine listening skills. Collaboration is beginning. Mutual trust can be the result.

Presentation Skills

Again, driven by the amount of information the buyer has, the seller needs even more. There are more presentation courses and more presentation software on the market now than ever before. The seller is still task driven. And the product is still the answer.

Negotiation Skills

With a well-informed buyer who is an integral part of the sales process, the seller needs the final proficiency: the ability to negotiate a sale. This new skill set brings in cost/benefit ratios and strategies for "winning." In fact, this skill set has superseded the old closing skills in the new sales methodologies.

Here's a summary of how Consultative sales works.

A typical salesperson learns product information, gets mailing lists and referrals, spends time making appointments
with prospects in order to sit face-to-face with them, and
frames their interaction around a win-win scenario. The
seller directs questions that seemingly examine buyer needs,
but in fact are leading the prospect to discover exactly why
she needs the seller's product. A consultation seems to be
happening, but the seller's ultimate goal is the buyer's
realization that she needs the seller's product. After the questioning process, the seller summarizes the buyer's environment and needs in relation to what the seller is selling.

Although Consultative selling uses questions—"probing" as
they call it—far more than Traditional sales, the basis of the questions is manipulation because the goal is the prospect's discovery
of her needs specifically in relation to the seller's product.

One of the best-known Consultative sales methodologies is
Sandler Sales. It has an approach similar to Buying Facilitation in
that it employs a questioning strategy to help a seller sell. I believe
that the questions this methodology uses, however, are based solely
on the seller finding a way to get the buyer to buy.

I have chosen some quotes from several segments of the Sandler Sales *Corporate Training and Development Program* audiocassette series to present the way Sandler sellers are taught to use
questions. Let me stress that in the Sandler Sales approach, respect
and collaboration are stated values, but in my opinion these values are implemented within a structure of manipulative strategies.
In fact, on the first tape of the series they state that the Sandler
approach will let the seller "gain a strategic and competitive edge
over the prospects."

On tape two, side *A*, the discussion concerns prospecting and
asking questions that may lead to a sale. Here is an example:
"Never answer an unasked question. Instead, stress those pains
that your prospect identified during the pain step. . . . Ask a question like, 'Mr. Prospect, we've discussed several features of this
product and it appears you have some interest in what we are dis-

cussing. Let me ask you a question: On a scale of zero to ten, zero being you have no interest in this product and ten being you see yourself already using this product, where are you?' If the prospect answers six or higher, you have a sold prospect."

Here's another set of questions from the same tape: "'Mr. Prospect, assuming I can deliver this product according to your specifications and assuming you can be comfortable with the investment, when do you see yourself using this product?' If the answer is 'as soon as possible,' make a commitment statement: 'Well, assuming that's the case, I assume you'll have to make a decision fairly soon, maybe even today. Is that a fair statement?'"

In both of the above scenarios, it is apparent to me that the questions are being used to create a need for the buyer to make a decision.

I'd also like to look at the SPIN Selling model put forth by Neil Rackham, since it's been such a successful approach for so long and one of the original Consultative sales approaches.

Rackham's research, detailed in *SPIN Selling*, is impressive and comes to many of the same conclusions I do: lots of questioning is necessary; rapport and relationship are vital, especially to larger ticket sales; closing techniques are not what cements a sale. But in my way of thinking, his four sets of questions show a very stylized sales approach, with the traditional behaviors handed in for updated ones based on the belief that "in almost every sales call you must convince your customer that you've something to offer." (p. 12)

Rackham's Investigative stage is comprised of the well-known SPIN model. Note that many of the behaviors he advocates are similar to Buying Facilitation, but quite different when seen through the filter of his beliefs around convincing.

> *Situation Questions:* Successful people tend to ask data-gathering questions about facts and background [such as] "How long have you had your present equipment?" or "Could you tell me about your company's growth plans?" (p. 17)

> *Problem Questions:* Explore problems, difficulties, and dissatisfactions in areas where the seller's product can help [such as]

"Is this operation difficult to perform?" or "Are you worried about the quality you get from your old machine?" (p. 17)

Implication Questions: Take a customer problem and explore its effects or consequences. . . . By asking Implication Questions, successful people help the customer understand a problem's seriousness or urgency [such as] "How will this problem affect your future profitability?" or "What effect does this reject rate have on customer satisfaction?" (p. 17)

Needs-payoff Questions: Get the customer to tell *you* the benefits that your solution could offer [such as] "Would it be useful to speed this operation by 10 percent?" or "If we could improve the quality of this operation, how would that help you?" (p. 17)

The questions are meant to get the prospect to understand for herself why she needs your product. For me, it remains seller-based and product-focused.

And this is why buyers don't tell sellers the truth.

Our questions have to bring buyers to places of discovery, not to *our* answers. I will present the complete questioning and listening methodology of Buying Facilitation in Section II.

I Know, You Don't

I believe that both Traditional and Consultative methodologies assume the following:

1. Because a prospect has a need in the area your product serves, your product is the answer.

2. Because a prospect could use your specific product to support a need, the prospect's internal cultural system is prepared to buy.

3. The prospect will buy if the seller uses the appropriate selling strategies.

Let's take a look at these assumptions.

Whatever approach you use, when you assume that your product is the answer, you are disrespecting a prospect's ability to discover her own answer. While your product may be *one* answer, if you believe it is the *only* answer, you are being "right." That makes me, as seller, right and you, as buyer, wrong: I know, you don't. When you try to convince prospects your way is the right way, you are telling them they are stupid. This is hardly new paradigm thinking, and a difficult way to create or maintain a trusting relationship.

When you assume that a prospect is ready, willing, and able to buy without taking into account the system in which she is making a buying decision, you are forgetting her need to collaborate with colleagues. Few buyers buy in a vacuum. Sellers, in need of forecasting dates for their sales managers, try to push the buyer into buying on the seller's time schedule, and again end up disrespecting the way the buyer buys.

When you assume people buy because you are a good sales person, you are minimizing a prospect's needs and superimposing your own need to sell.

Because the values in the new business paradigm are different, salespeople need a new and different set of beliefs and skills. In the next chapter, we will go through the beliefs and skills of Buying Facilitation and see how they support our being servants to our buyers.

SKILL SET #3:

Traditional Sales and Consultative Sales

To decide whether you want to make changes in your selling style as a result of the approach offered in this book, ask yourself these questions:

- ☐ What are the basic beliefs you hold about sales?

- ☐ How you are selling now? What is your general style?

☐ What outcome do you have in mind prior to entering a dialogue?

☐ How well does that work for you? Does it give you the response you seek? Under what conditions does it work? Not work?

☐ What part of the outcome or interaction would you want changed? How would you approach making changes? What additional skills do you currently have that you could substitute for the ones you think need to be changed?

☐ Review your sales beliefs, skills, and behaviors again. Note any that feel uncomfortable but that you do as part of your accustomed selling approach.

☐ How do these skills and behaviors compare with those you use in daily communication when not in a work setting? Which ones do you believe are essential to your work? Nonessential but just habit? What's the difference?

☐ What would need to happen for you to be willing to change those approaches to be consistent with those you use when not in a work setting?

☐ How would you use the skills offered in this book to support you?

Chapter 5

The Seller as Servant

Until now, selling has been seller-based and product-focused without taking into account the full complement of a buyer's needs. This has been true of every sales approach regardless of industry, product, or sales environment. Although the Consultative approaches do address buyers' needs more than the Traditional approaches, they still assume the product is the answer, and it's the seller's job to learn the best way to direct the prospect toward the product.

In Buying Facilitation, it's the seller's job to help prospects discern what they need in our area of expertise and assist them in figuring out how to align the solution with the needs of the decision-making body. Let's take a look at Buying Facilitation and see how it will assist you in serving your clients and thus serving yourself, as well as in making money and selling product.

Buying Facilitation: The Beliefs

Buying Facilitation is

Service-Based

Solution-Focused

Relationship-Based

It looks like this:

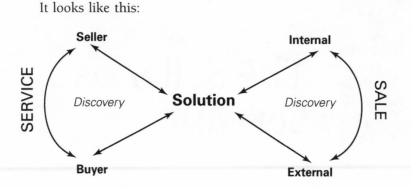

The main beliefs are:

1. ***The prospect has ultimate control over the outcome of the interaction.***

As one of my clients says, reminiscent of President Clinton's 1992 presidential campaign, "It's the buyer, stupid." It is amazing to me that sellers don't act as if they understand they cannot make a sale without a buyer giving them a check. Given that the buyer has the ultimate control, what must our job as seller be? How do we make money? How do we sell product? And how do we carry out our job?

2. ***The seller's job is to support the prospective buyer's needs.***

To switch from the belief that the seller has the answers to the belief that the seller's job is to support and facilitate the buyer gives the seller a totally new job description. It actually makes the job of salesperson much easier. All a seller needs now is the questions. Of course, product knowledge is necessary, but not to the same extent it once was, especially on the first call. When the interaction was task-based, the seller had to have the answers. Now that the job can be relationship-based and solution-focused, the answers aren't the point.

3. ***The prospective buyer knows what he needs and can solve his own problems with the support of the seller's questions.***

Information isn't always stored sequentially in our brains, which means it is sometimes difficult to retrieve. In fact, when people say "I don't know," they really mean, "I don't know where in my brain that information is stored nor how to retrieve it." If they really didn't know, they would stare blankly. When you say to someone who has just professed to not know something, "Make a guess," he will come up with the answer. At that point, he does a brain search instead of looking in his normal place. *A seller can actually teach a buyer how to scan his brain for his own answers.*

4. *People buy only when they cannot solve their problem with their own internal resources; then they seek an external solution.*

It has never been about the product or the seller. You can have the best product and the best sales pitch in the world. If it's not the right time or the right place or the right set of circumstances, there's no reason to buy. And buyers have to be ready and willing to change—that's the big one.

5. *Sellers will find the right people to buy their product independent of their need to sell.*

The only reason a buyer buys is that he needs the product. When a seller puts aside his selling patterns to support a buyer's buying patterns, he only needs to find people who need the product to make a sale. Sure, you have to put the time in to make the calls and visits, but the ultimate sale is not dependent upon how a seller "sells."

6. *Prospective buyers and sellers trust each other and are honest with each other, communicating in a "We Space" uniquely their own.*

When a buyer understands that the seller is there to serve, there is no reason not to trust and receive the offered support. The seller must take the responsibility to create an environment of trust, however, and ensure that the buyer and seller are aligned on the same side of the table, both knowing the ultimate goal is to support the buyer in getting his needs met. I call this environment a "We Space"—the place where the two people involved in an interaction, the "I's" if you will, meet as an entity in the middle and constitute a unique duo—the "We." Until now, sales has been the "I" of the seller seeking the "I" of the buyer, rather than creating a "We." I'll be speaking more about "We Space" in chapter 8.

7. *Prospective buyers have the answers, sellers have the questions.*

Once we understand the buyer has the answers, the seller's job becomes one of helping the buyer sequence the information in his brain so he can see his way clear to solve his own problems. I give the seller the job of maintaining the structure—the direction and context—of the buyer/seller interaction. The buyer's job is to generate the content. Until now, it has been the opposite, with the seller taking control of the content of the interaction and losing the pathway to the sale. I will be discussing this thoroughly in chapter 9.

8. *Prospective buyers know what they need, but prefer to work collaboratively with sellers in win-win situations that support each getting their needs met.*

Interdependence is the deal. Once sellers believe that buyers really do have their own answers, it becomes their job to offer buyers their skills and support in a way recognized by the buyers as supportive (more on this in chapter 9). The product may be an answer; it may not. But the seller will structure the interaction to support the buyer's discovery of how to meet his own needs. The seller becomes an integral part of the buyer's decision-making team. In the Buying Facilitation method, the seller is placed on the same side of the table as the buyer in order to serve the buyer more valuably. Because of the seller's support, the buyer now has a clear view of the solution—whether it be the seller's product or an alternative.

In order for a prospect to make a decision about purchasing the seller's product, there must be a clear view of the product *at the time the prospect discovers he needs an external resource.* If the product is introduced before the prospect understands what he needs, he will actually be repelled by the product, and his personal values around his ability to solve his own problems will be offended. There should be nothing—and no one—between the prospect and the product. The prospect has a direct line to the product if it provides the solution to his problem.

Buying Facilitation: The Skills

Here are the skills we need for the new methodology.

Ability to Move between Communication Choice Points to Ensure Understanding and Continued Rapport

This is the most difficult part for sellers new to Buying Facilitation: knowing what to say, how, and when, without resorting to old selling patterns. *Since the seller must support the way a buyer buys, using any tried and true communication patterns will negate the intent.* By using no selling patterns at all, the seller can work with a buyer's buying patterns and get into rapport on the buyer's terms. This creates trust; buyers can tell the difference immediately.

Questioning and Listening

Our questions have to bring a buyer to a place of discovery, not to our answers. Our listening ferrets out the areas a buyer needs to examine to fully understand his situation. We are not listening in order to notice a thinking glitch we can use to sell into.

Responsibility for Collaborative Communication

Until now, sellers have not taken responsibility for the interaction, just for knowing their product and having a unique sales approach (knowing how to handle objections, for example). In fact, whenever the interaction has not gone the way the seller believes it should go, he blames the buyer for getting it wrong. Now, with Buying Facilitation, sellers have the responsibility to create the structure of the communication. The buyer not only may not know how to do it, but he certainly will not have the desire to do it with a stranger. Once the seller creates an environment in which a true collaboration can take place, a buyer is usually delighted to enter into it.

Ability to Shift Communication Skills to Support the Beliefs, Needs, and Culture of the Buyer

It's a tough job, but somebody has to do it. Remember: "It's the buyer, stupid." And the buying decision process is the only way to the product, *if* the product is the answer. If it's not, the seller has still supported the buyer in discovering how best to get his needs met. As we saw in the brief example with the office supply company in chapter 4, it can take less than five minutes to create this discovery—less time than it takes to attempt to get an appointment.

Trust, Rapport, and Respect

Again, the buyer doesn't know how or why to create an environment of trust and respect with a stranger. It's the seller's responsibility. Once a buyer enters a "We Space" with the seller and begins to reap the benefits of the seller's questions, he will begin to take his share of responsibility for maintaining the relationship. On the first call, however, it's up to the seller to create the rapport. *Remember: there are three ways to make a sale: Rapport, Rapport, and Rapport.* No matter how good your product is, how good your questions are, if you are out of rapport with your buyer there won't be a sale. There is always another product and another salesperson similar enough to you for the buyer not to have to be in an uncomfortable situation.

In summary, here's how Buying Facilitation works.

A seller learns about the product, and spends equal time learning relationship-building and communication skills. A seller gets names from appropriate lists or uses the Yellow Pages to find potential buyers. The seller uses the telephone as the main qualifying tool, trusting that through the interaction both people can discover whether or not they should move forward and how. That "meeting" takes place if the buyer decides it's in his best interests to do so. The seller creates a collaborative environment: he sets up a win-win interaction, with the seller in control of the structure and direction of the conversation and the buyer in control of the content. The seller uses the questioning process to assist the buyer in looking at the current environment in which the seller's product is being/could be used. The questions then focus on helping the buyer discover what's missing.

Once missing pieces start coming forth, the seller changes his questioning to assist the buyer in looking at the buyer's own internal resources to meet the needs. When internal resources can be found, the seller might then ask for names of referrals who might need his product and end the relationship there. When internal resources cannot be found, the buyer begins asking about the seller's product and how it might answer the needs.

Only at the point where the buyer is clear he cannot meet his needs through internal resources does the seller move to the product explanation, and he only discusses those areas where there is a fit. At this point, the buyer is in control of the questions and structure; the seller is in control of the content. Once the product is described, the seller then asks the buyer how he would like to go forward. This includes: what the buyer needs from the seller in order to know if the product is the right one; whether the relationship between the buyer and the seller is working for the buyer; if the buyer thinks the buyer's and seller's companies can work together; and how the seller can contribute to the buyer's decision-making process.

The Seller as Servant

To take on any of these new beliefs or behaviors, change is necessary. But change is difficult. The overriding ideas of sales have persisted until now. In the nicest ways, with the nicest people, with the highest principles in mind, sales has promoted disrespect.

Because we in America are not trained to serve, or even think multidimensionally, the split between task and relationship, mind and spirit persists. Sales, the preeminent business skill, has assumed the ultimate insult: to serve itself.

It's time to grow beyond our cultural narcissism and serve each other. I propose that the seller become the servant to the buyer. When sellers hear me use the word *servant* in relation to their jobs, they often wince, so let me explain this a bit through a story.

A man died. When he "came to" and realized he was no longer living, he looked around and found an angel sitting by him.

"Would you like a tour of the grounds?" the angel asked.

The angel led the man around. The first room he came into was a darkened room with beautiful candlelight and many people sitting around a bubbling pot of delicious-smelling stew. Oh, what a smell! Just like mother's kitchen on a cold, rainy day.

"Where am I?" the man asked the angel.

"You're in hell."

"But how can I be in hell with such an amazing stew?"

"Watch."

The man looked again and noticed the people were severely emaciated, although they each held the handle of a six-foot-long spoon. As he continued to watch he saw that occasionally one person would maneuver the spoon into the pot, take out a spoonful of delicious-looking stew, and attempt to maneuver the bowl of the spoon into his mouth, only to watch the food end up on the floor due to the length of the handle.

The people were starving, with as much food as they needed just a spoonful away.

"What does heaven look like?" the man asked the angel.

The angel brought him to another room, which looked exactly the same as the first. The dim light, the people sitting around, the long spoons, the delicious stew. But there was a difference. These people were well fed and happy. There was laughter in the room. The man watched while the people took turns maneuvering their six-foot-long spoons into the stew. But instead of trying to get the spoonful of stew into their own mouths they were feeding each other. And all had food.

Serving Our Clients and Ourselves

This is my perception of service: by serving our clients we serve ourselves. We all get our needs met, and we all have abundance.

It's time for the seller to become a servant—to the buyer, to the company, to the culture. And in return, he will be served—by the buyer, the company, the culture. Again, it's interdependence: win-win or no deal.

In Buying Facilitation, it is the seller's job, as servant, to lead the buyer through the process of discovering what precisely the buyer needs to know in order to make the best decision possible. *I believe that buyers know what they need. Buyers would have fixed the problem if they knew how and why and when.* We must assume they didn't see a clear pathway to the answer.

The seller must serve the prospect, not the product. And buyers know the difference. Here's an example of one way I used Buying Facilitation.

I was called to meet with a group at a large hardware company to discuss the possibility of assisting them with a new marketing directive. By the time I got there, the team had decided they were doing fine and they didn't need an external resource. I was told I could present for ten minutes since I had taken the time to visit them.

"I don't present. I just ask questions," I said.

They all laughed good-naturedly, and told me to go ahead with my questions for the ten allotted minutes. I began asking questions about their current environment, where they were going, how they were going to get there with the resources they had in place, what internal resources could supply the missing pieces, what was still missing, what criteria they would use to complete any missing pieces, and how the team would adjust to working with outside people where external resources were needed.

One and one-half hours later, my questions had led them to look into areas they hadn't considered, and they discovered a need they hadn't noticed that they could not fill internally. They talked among themselves and decided they would be willing to look for an external solution. They asked me if I could support the particular problem that had emerged. I walked away with a job—not because I sold them something, but because they bought. They recognized for themselves what they needed, how they needed to buy, and how they needed to bring a resource onto the team. My facilitative questions supported them in discovering that their internal resources were inadequate, a fact I had no way of knowing when I entered the room. But my job was to serve.

I assisted them in discovering the best use of their own resources, and in the process they discovered missing pieces. I did not discuss my product or assume it might be an answer until they asked me specifically if I could supply the missing piece. Because I did not go to the meeting to push a product or with the assumption that I had answers for them, I gained their trust and became part of the team. By meeting their criteria for adding resources to their existent system, I became a supplier. It was win-win, with no sales cycle.

Creating a Win-Win Environment

The shift I am describing is from salesperson as authority to salesperson as servant. Win-lose no longer needs to reign when you can make more money and sell your product appropriately through ethically based methods that support the integrity of each individual in the process. You must work from the assumption that it's your job—in fact, your *responsibility*—to create win-win relationships with respect and integrity. And in return, you will have buyers who will work with you in trusting, creative relationships.

People who train with me are amazed at how easily I form relationships with prospects: I just *be* with them. And since people only buy what they need, the way they need it, from people they trust, it doesn't matter how useful or powerful or wonderful my product is if people don't trust that I have their best interests at heart. Ultimately, all I have is *me* and my ability to serve. *The product or service for which they pay me is the deliverable.*

You Can Be Successful

People have found that Buying Facilitation increases sales dramatically, decreases turnover, increases work enjoyment, and aligns sellers' personal values with their sales jobs: and sellers are closing three to five times more business. One recent statistic I can share concerns a group of telemarketers I trained. The initial group of seventeen sellers closed twenty sales in the seven months prior

to their training with me. In the four weeks following their training, the eleven remaining sellers (six were redeployed) closed four-
teen sales. In the next four weeks, they closed fifteen sales with a
revenue equaling their entire year-to-date income.

Once the numbers were all in, there was a two hundred percent increase in sales in the eight weeks following the training.
Here are some additional reasons why the approach is so effective:

1. You get to, or get the name of, the appropriate person—
    either the qualified buyer or a member of the decision-mak-
    ing body—on the first call. You don't spend days, weeks, or
    months trying to reach Mr. Jones, chief executive officer or
    department head, when all of his decisions are made by Mr.
    Smith who is easily reachable. How much time do you save
    when you get to the right person immediately?

2. You get into rapport immediately. Since people generally
    only buy from people they like, you are on firm footing
    from your first moment.

3. You are able to lead potential buyers through a questioning
    sequence that will lead them to define the following, all on
    the first call!:

    ▪ Where they are at.

    ▪ Where they are going.

    ▪ How they are going to get there.

    ▪ What has stopped them until now.

    ▪ How they need to work with a decision-making body.

    ▪ What the cultural issues and problems are.

    ▪ What criteria they will use to choose an external solution
    or supplier.

    ▪ How they will know that you and your product might be
    an answer.

People using the Buying Facilitation method have found
over and over again that a six-month sales cycle easily gets reduced
to six weeks (where feasible), using the phone as the original

qualifying tool. (While face-to-face meetings are necessary in a large number of cases, it's often not necessary to make an in-person visit to qualify when you use the Buying Facilitation questions on the initial call. In fact, you might consider only going to visit those people ready and willing to close.)

In an average sales cycle (six months, for example) several weeks, if not months, are spent getting to the qualified buyer: finding the right person, waiting for a response, and chasing down the person for a decision. Several more days or weeks are spent sending and receiving the necessary information and documentation. More weeks and months are spent waiting while the team or buyer makes decisions. Much of this waiting, this void, is eliminated when using Buying Facilitation.

In general, the sales cycle will be shorter because necessary information will come to light sooner, as will previously not-thought-of questions. The seller-buyer interaction will be a primary source of creativity.

You now have a better understanding of where we have been as sellers and where we need to go. To implement the beliefs inherent in a sales methodology based on collaboration, respect, and serving requires new skills. In section II, we will explore these new skills in light of how and why people buy.

SKILL SET #4:

Taking Responsibility to Serve

- [ ] Consider your current thinking about the responsibility you hold in your sales job. Is it for your company? yourself? your job? your clients? your prospects? your team? your family? How does that express itself in your daily activities?

- [ ] Does that level and focus of responsibility affect your bottom line? How?

- [ ] When you think of being in service to your prospects and clients, what does that mean to you?

- [ ] What happens when you think about giving up the authority that has traditionally been part of a seller's job?

- [ ] Do you currently present? How do you choose which prospects to present to? How do you choose which materials to present? What are your results?

- [ ] What would you need to know or do differently in order to consider taking a different level of responsibility with your prospects and clients?

II

The Components of Buying Facilitation

In this section, I will walk you through the components of Buying Facilitation: how and why people buy and how you can support a buyer's discovery through the Buying Decision Funnel. In addition, I will show you how you can gain the skills necessary to do the following:

1. Create an interdependent environment between seller and buyer.

2. Create communication that brings the prospective buyer to a decision on an internal or external solution.

3. Close appropriate sales quickly.

The Skill Sets will give you a way to practice each new tool before going on to the next. There is a lot of practical information here; use the parts you find easiest first, then add new skills as needed.

Chapter 6

The Factors in the Buying Decision Process

Much has been written about the skills sellers need in order to "make a sale." In this chapter, I will address my understanding of the thinking process buyers must go through in considering whether or not they need to buy.

I've been in the sales profession since 1979, when I tired of being a poor social worker for the city of New York and went to Wall Street. At that time, I innocently walked into the fiftieth floor corner office of the executive vice president of human resources at Merrill Lynch, Pierce, Fenner, and Smith and announced to this surprised stranger that I wanted him to hire me. He did.

Merrill had what was considered to be the best sales training in the business: a one-month program that taught everything from wearing high socks (for the men) to not wearing dangling earrings (for the women). We were taught Traditional and Consultative methods with plenty of phone-skills training as a prospecting tool. I learned well. I opened 210 accounts in my first six months as a rookie in a bear market. My experience in London, however, as both a seller and an entrepreneur, led to my discovery of a key piece in the sales process, a piece never taught in sales training— the process buyers go through before reaching a decision to buy.

Do You Want to Sell or Do You Want to Have Someone Buy?

In my training programs, one of the first questions I ask sellers is whether they believe there is a sale without a buyer. To a person, they all agree: no buyer, no sale. Then I play a game with them. I put an invisible widget in my hand and invite participants to provide a reason for me to buy it. To make it easy, I offer them the option to decide what it is. "You can make it be *anything* you want it to be—and I'm an easy sell." They go around the room with this problem. Each person finds ways to convince me that what they have in their hand is the perfect item for me, starting conversations with: "Hello, Sharon Drew, I've got something here I think you'll like . . ." and they proceed to try to convince me that they have the answer to my life's desires.

No one thinks to ask me what I need! Even in a classroom setting, where they have already agreed there is no sale without a buyer, where the product can be anything they want it to be, where all possible choices are available to them, *the sellers choose what they want to sell rather than find out what I need to buy!* They assume they are responsible to create an answer for me. But **people buy only when they can't fill their own needs** with the resources at hand. When a salesperson approaches a prospect with a potential fix to a problem, there is no appreciation for what a prospect must deal with in order to change how she is currently handling that problem.

The course participants do with me what they've been taught to do: figure out how to position the product, decide the outcome before going in, and establish enough rapport to make a pitch and ask opening questions. Once participants recognize what I'm suggesting, they become quiet. The skills of sales have not traditionally included the buyer's decision-making process, at least not at the conceptual level. Sellers are generally happy to extend their thinking to how and why people buy. Until now, it just wasn't part of the job.

SKILL SET #5:

Understanding Why People Buy

Remember a situation in which you were convinced that your prospect needed your product, but was not responding positively. Try to remember how you reacted to the opportunity to sell your product.

☐ Did you assume that you had the answer? That your product was it?

☐ Did you assume that the prospect was wrong? That she just needed to know what your product could do and then she'd understand that your product was her solution?

☐ How did you interact with your prospect when she didn't agree with you? What thoughts went through your mind? Did your thoughts come across to the prospect? In what form?

☐ How did you create objections? What type of objections do you normally get? Is there a pattern to them?

☐ In what ways do you alter or become creative around solutions if/when you notice that your product is not the perfect solution for the prospect?

The White Sock Drawer and the Missing Orange Sock—

Or, How Do People Decide to Buy?

I've created an allegory based on artificial intelligence guru Roger Schank's *Tell Me a Story* in order to illustrate some tools, tips, and techniques I've learned to use to assist buyers in their thinking and decision-making processes. Though far fetched and somewhat "creative," the story offers an easy way to understand how and why we have to use questions to help a prospect discover what, if anything, she needs to buy. Here's my tale:

In my room I have a huge dresser. I am an active sports person and change socks several times during a day, so one of my larger drawers houses all of my white socks. Because I wear them under jeans, with workout clothes, with jogging shoes, and with boots, nobody really sees them. So if they don't match—given some are grayer or yellower or holier or longer or shorter than others—it's not a big deal. They are just thrown into the drawer and I grab for any two when I need them.

In another, smaller drawer, I have my colored socks. These are neatly paired: red with red, green with green. These socks are usually for show and worn only occasionally. I wear them with matching shirts or sweaters or dress trousers. They must match or I won't wear the outfit. (Crazy? Maybe, but it's *my* story.)

Let's say I go golfing annually to Pebble Beach and I have a great orange shirt to wear on the golf course. That means I have a pair of identical orange socks to match the shirt.

If a salesperson were to call me up and tell me she had a special on socks, my obvious mental reference would be to think about my large supply of white socks and tell her I had no need. (When we are asked general questions, our brains automatically default to the most familiar references. Therefore, a seller with the best socks in the world would have nothing to sell me.)

But if she asked me what specific types of socks I had, I would have to bring to mind the two drawers and explain about the two categories of socks. I would happily go into an explanation of how I grab my white socks, then go into an explanation of my colored sock drawer. If she wanted to go into specifics—and given I'm not so familiar with my colored socks as I am with my white socks since I don't use them as often—I'd have to go to my room to open my drawer and name all the different colors I have. Here's a red pair that I wear with this amazing shirt. And these yellow ones my son brought me from Rome. And the orange ones . . . oh my, there is only one orange sock here! Gosh.

This is where many sellers go wrong. If they are able to get to the missing piece—and the majority of sellers are so busy pitching socks and taking care of their own needs to sell that they don't even get as far as the colored sock drawer—they go on to assume that their orange socks are the answer. Yet there are several potential scenarios here.

What if I no longer play golf? Then I won't need any orange socks. What if I just got a multicolored sweater for Christmas, and I don't have nearly enough socks? What if I won't be golfing any longer but have an orange ski suit and need orange wool socks instead of cotton socks? And what if my family owns a department store, and I can get all the socks I want wholesale?

How We Store Information

For much of my thinking about thinking and the question-development process, which I'll be discussing in great detail throughout the book, I reference Roger Schank, who explains these things in far more sophisticated terms. From his research, he has found that our brains store information in indices. In *Tell Me a Story* he says:

> The problem always reduces to search. A mind must be able to find what it needs to find, and it must know it has found it. . . . If there is no way to find [it], it might as well not exist. (p. 84)

Basically, we store most of our information in a large general index—the white sock drawer as I'm calling it. As the information gets more specifically defined, it transfers into smaller, more specialized indices—the colored sock drawer—that have more specific but less-used information. In order for us to find this highly qualified information, we have to know where to search for it. Somehow, we have to be asked the right questions to get to the right index, because *we only search for infrequently used information when we need different information from what is most readily available.*

It is not until a prospect recognizes that there is a problem and searches for and finds the right index that she will know how or when or with what to solve the problem, or that she will choose to add an additional resource to her current environment. Rarely are people aware of all of this up front.

Prospects Only Buy If They Can't Fix What They Have

Let's look at the buying process. Before people will consider buying they must

- recognize there is something missing;
- verbalize, visualize, or in some other way understand the steps needed to get to a solution;
- explore all possible ways to solve the problem;
- understand how to support existing personnel and systems during the disruption an external resource creates.

Change presents disruption of the status quo. Teams, companies, families, and individuals—the decision makers in the buying cycle—would much rather fix what they've got than bring a foreign element into the system.

When a seller assumes that people will buy because she creates or finds a need and presents a case for her product, she is playing God.

Discovery: Or I Think I Don't Need Anything, Thank You

In *The Creative Attitude*, Roger Schank states:

> In order to want to know, one must find things one needs to know. You can't look for explanations, for new ideas, or for new generalizations unless the old ones have been found inadequate to account for some anomaly. (p. 12)

In other words, if a prospect's current status—her Present Situation as I call it—seems just fine, she has no need to look further. Two things can affect her thinking: either a change in the environment can cause her to seek a solution or she may realize that although the environment is the same, it's not functioning optimally. In either case, she needs to go through a process to find a solution and that will involve a brain search.

If change is imminent, there will be more of a push to find a solution than if there is no immediate need. Most of your clients know they need a solution and are searching for the best alternative. Yet the Buying Facilitation process uncovers many undiscovered problems, which are accidents waiting to happen. Rarely do I speak with a prospect who is totally happy with her Present Situation and unwilling to look at improving it in some way. When all seems to be fine, and I ask, "Are there any conditions under which you would consider supplementing your current service with an additional resource?" people think about a wish list. And often people who are not actively seeking a solution take another look.

Now that you know your job is to bring a prospect to the colored sock drawer to help her determine what's missing and what's not, let's look at why people decide to buy.

The Problem Space: Viewing the Parameters That Hold the Problem

It is important to understand that a problem your product or service might address is only one element in the broader picture, that I call the Problem Space. On the next page is an illustration of the problem, the Problem Space, and the Solution Space.

A Problem Space in a business setting is made up of the roles, rules, time factors, politics, sociology, budgets—the entire culture—of the company, and is defined in relation to who and what resides within

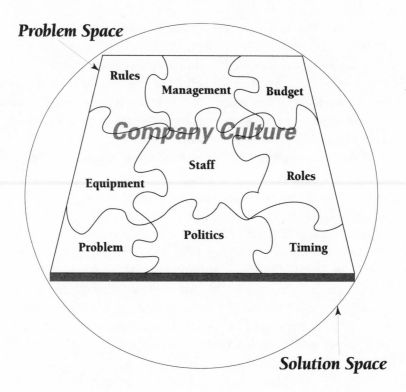

it. The elements within the Problem Space are so unique to each business that it is virtually impossible for an outsider to understand how the elements interact.

Most buyers cannot get a full view of a problem from their vantage point within the system—they often cannot see symptoms, causes, and possible solutions. Offering a product, which may or may not be the answer, is meaningless if there is no place for that product within the Problem Space. (We will explore the discovery process in Skill Set #6.)

As sellers, one of your tasks is to assist your prospects in understanding how their problem supports and is supported by the larger system. Indeed, people will only add resources when their Problem Space is defined and found lacking. They might not even look to see if there is a problem—or what, if anything, needs to be fixed or purchased—until there is a fire to put out, and even then defining the parameters of the Problem Space is not an easy task.

Since understanding the Problem Space is so important to a prospect solving her internal problem and potentially working with you to make a purchasing decision, I'd like to spend some time leading you through the thought process that helps prospects examine the Problem Space boundaries.

What Needs to Change?

The easiest place to start is with the identified problem—the need for more hardware or the desire for more insurance coverage, for example. Why isn't the status quo still okay? Something must have happened to make the existing solution inadequate. The reasons for the inadequacy must be addressed, one at a time. The identified problem begins to show up as a piece of a string of other changes: staffing, reorganizations, or budgets, for example. More questions beginning with "how" and "why" and "what" will help to reveal the pieces of a larger picture. All of these pieces, which may appear to be peripheral to the problem, carry some kind of weight, with some elements more important than others. Even a simple problem like a toothache resides in a Problem Space bigger than the toothache itself. You have no way of knowing which elements carry more weight than others until you ask. Here's an example:

When working with a customer service department in a major steel company, I noticed much anger and disruption among team members. Long-term employees—upwards of twenty years—were becoming ill and entering the hospital, getting to work late, fighting with teammates. I was working with this group because customer complaints were on the rise, but I walked into a problem much bigger than anyone had imagined. I spent some time gathering information to get a clear picture of the Problem Space.

There had been a major reorganization several months before my arrival. The initial problem was getting people moved to the reorganization sites in the most efficient way possible: moving money was offered and travel arrangements were made through a company office. People were moved to various sites around the country after having been in their homes for many years. While there was disruption, the move occurred on time and everyone ended up where they were supposed to be without a hitch.

But no one had been asked what they needed, how they felt, what hardships their families faced, or who was left behind. The move was accomplished as a task: the job was to reorganize. People's lives had not been factored into the problem, which was now much bigger than just moving people. The initial problem of moving people efficiently now included a Problem Space filled with unhappy, unhealthy people, jobs not being done effectively, customer service problems not being handled appropriately, and increased customer complaints.

I spoke with people and discovered a very simple solution. At my suggestion, the customer service director called a large meeting and *listened* to people. They wanted to be heard—to gripe and complain, even to cry. Some had left behind teenagers in their last year of high school. Others left dying family members, or animals, or best friends. They needed to go through a grieving process and had not been offered a chance. The director spent time with them, recognized the problem, apologized deeply, and much to his credit, cried with them. The people were heard and acknowledged. The problems dissipated.

In this instance, the customer service director had not understood the size of his problem until there was a major "fire." The eventual solution encompassed more elements and effort than if he had situated the initial problem within a complete Problem Space.

At the outset, he might have been led through a questioning sequence that would have begun with the need to move the people and continued through all of the "people" issues that might come up during a move. Some questions might have been the following:

- How do we see this move happening on an individual basis?

- What might be the concerns and issues each person must address?

- How will we or they address those elements in their lives that might not easily fit into our reorganization?
- What do we have in place, as a company, to support these issues?
- How will we advertise this support and offer it to the people?
- How will we know if people are having difficulties, so we can be flexible around the type of support we are offering?
- How will we know when it is all handled effectively?

By starting with the problem and moving from there to the surrounding issues, the Problem Space becomes clear to the buyer. Remember: *The buyer has the answers. You can't make a sale without a buyer.*

Solutions and Solution Space

Once you have supported the buyer in discovering the parameters of the Problem Space, you must then support her in examining a solution whose defined area—the Solution Space—is bigger than, and encompasses, the Problem Space.

For instance, in the above example, the initial solution was to bring me in to teach better communication tools to the customer service representatives to solve the problem of increased customer complaints. Once the Problem Space was fully defined as including personal issues left over from the move and not just customer complaints, the Solution Space was easy to spot: listen to the issues, hear the people on a personal level, get management involved, fix any lingering issues so people can once again be happy in their jobs. But there was no way to discover the complexities of the solution or the Solution Space until the entire Problem Space had been defined and each internal element examined.

Too often an inadequate solution is directed toward a problem.

Sellers, especially, often assume their product will solve a problem and don't take into account all of the issues involved.

I had an embarrassing experience involving a too-small Solution Space at an in-house customer service training in a major union shop.

While on the floor with the customer service representatives, I noticed they would forsake all the skills they were learning when they received a call from a union member. Believing in a "We Space," I spent the better part of the next day teaching the reps about aligning with their unionized coworkers.

The next day I was called into the manager's office with one of the inside sales reps to relate the story of what had happened following my training the previous day. Apparently when a union man called to tell the rep he had a problem getting a product delivered on the promised date, she replied, "I guess we have a problem. What can we do to make it work for the customer?" (I must admit when I heard her respond this way I was quite proud of the rep for learning so quickly.) Ten minutes later the union member and his boss, the head of the trucking union, marched into the manager's office demanding the rep be fired.

"What is this *we* shit? Get her outta here."

This was the first time I realized the difference between a problem and the Problem Space, and it was a hard lesson. I hadn't known the parameters of the Problem Space—the rules and idiosyncrasies of the union–inside sales rep relationship—and my solution wasn't big enough. I thought I had something to "sell" without ascertaining what my client needed to "buy." I did not have enough perspective to view the problem in its entirety and in fact became part of the problem.

In defining a Solution Space, both the central and the peripheral issues must be addressed with great specificity for the prospect to be willing to look toward, and understand the need for, a solution. Again, until or unless the prospect is certain she cannot get her own needs met with what she has in place, she will not seek an external solution. *People buy only when they can't fill their own needs.*

It may be some time before you actually begin to believe that your product or service may in fact not be the answer. After all, there have been centuries of history of sales techniques that support you believing otherwise. Begin the thinking and just notice what happens when you introduce the new questions into your daily sales calls.

SKILL SET #6:

The Problem and Solution Spaces

Think of prospecting calls you have initiated. Remember how you went about discovering the prospect's needs.

☐ How free from your need to sell are your investigative questions? How do your needs going into the interaction color the responses you receive? the quality of the information offered?

☐ How do you know what types of information to extract from a prospect regarding the identified problem?

☐ What questions do you ask? How do you think of formulating these questions? How do you know which questions to ask— or not ask?

☐ How do you know that the quality of information you seek regarding a prospect's real needs is within the answers you receive? How do you go about getting the highest quality information?

☐ Do you work with the problem only? Do you incorporate the Problem Space in your thinking? How would you do that? What would you need to know or do differently in order to bring in the concept of Problem Space to your sales calls?

☐ What needs to happen for you to find all of the issues that need to be brought into the Solution Space? To differentiate the solution from the Solution Space?

Chapter 7

How People Buy

When you use selling patterns, *you are actually restricting the information exchange to those topics you've decided need to be addressed.* In fact, you can use the parameters of the Buying Decision Funnel, which we'll be discussing later in this chapter, to contain the issues to be addressed and keep the buyer within the boundaries of the problem, Problem Space, solution, and Solution Space. You are switching your job from containing the conversation to comply with your need to sell, to containing the conversation to support a detailed examination of what goes into a buying decision, given the prospect's unique environment.

In this chapter, we'll be examining the Buying Decision Funnel and the questions buyers must consider before deciding on a solution. I've also chosen examples from six disparate industries to give you ideas of how to use the Funnel in many situations.

How Sellers Keep Prospects from Buying

Because **people buy using their own buying patterns, not a seller's selling patterns,** the use of an opening pitch is one of the primary obstructions to sales.

Here's a great example of how opening pitches are more for the seller than for the prospect. I received a call from a not-so-successful salesperson recently.

> "Hello. This is Sharon Drew."
> "Hi! Ms. Morgen?
> "Yes. Who's this?"
> "My name is Steven Phillips from X Winery and I'm calling to tell you about our company. We are a seventy-year-old winery, founded by . . ."
> "Why are you telling me this?"
> "We think it's important for you to know what type of company we are, where we came from, who our founders were . . ."
> "Why?" I was definitely feeling mischievous by this point.
> "What?"
> "Why?"
> "Why what?"
> "Why do I need to know about your winery?"
> "So you can know the quality of company behind the wine you are buying."
> "I'm not buying wine."
> "What?"
> "I'm allergic to wine. I get violently ill when I drink it. I haven't had any for fifteen years."
> "So why did you call?"
> "I left a message to speak with Steven Jones. I am discussing sales training with him."
> "Oh. They gave the message to the wrong Steven. Sorry. I'll have Steven Jones call you back."

While just a fun example, it points out the direction a call takes as the result of the way the seller approaches the opening pitch.

One of the basic tools sellers learn is how to set the stage for interaction with the prospect. Opening pitches were created on the assumption that if the seller positions the product appropriately, chances increase that the prospect will buy it. This assumption has deterred more people from buying than any other: it is the embodiment of seller-based and product-focused selling. It assumes the buyer wants to listen to the information the seller is offering, and is ready, willing, and able to buy.

During my stint as an entrepreneur, I learned that there are fairly universal issues people must address in order to find a solution to a business problem. I believe the sequence people need to follow in order to address the issues is pretty standard also.

The Stages of Decision Making

In order to make a decision to buy a new product or service, not only must a prospect have a clear understanding that what is in place no longer works, but also that the current systems—political, management, financial, team/personnel—will accept the fix and remain intact.

Change presents some disruption of the status quo. Teams, companies, families, and individuals—the decision makers in the buying cycle—would rather fix what they've got than bring a foreign element into the system. Usually at least one-half of the decision-making process is devoted to trying to fix the problem within the Problem Space. Prior to my experience as an entrepreneur, I never made appropriate allowances for the machinations the prospect goes through to avoid using an external resource. Once I became a business owner myself, I recognized how difficult it is to change the system: the people issues, finances, and politics place external solutions far down on the list of favorite choices.

From both experiences—seller and entrepreneur—I've come up with a ten-step process that I think addresses the major issues a buyer must think through before making a decision to use an external solution.

1. *Survey the current environment.*

What's in place now? How did it get that way? What systems does the current environment support?

2. Discern where the environment needs to be in the future.

Why is it not there yet? What has stopped that from happening? What's stopping the team (or company or family or individual—the decision makers) from solving the problem *now?*

3. Check internal resources.

What is obviously in place *now* that could fix the problem? Why isn't it being used?

4. Sort out what specifically is missing to get from here to there.

How did that happen?

5. Decision makers must do a thorough examination of potential internal fixes.

People would much rather fix what they have than change the system. Decision makers must search each element of the system thoroughly to find an internal solution. **People buy only when they can't fill their own needs.**

6. Agree to search for an external solution.

Decision makers must agree to an action plan and a direction once they know that existing internal systems can't fix the problem. How does the group go about deciding how to go forward in agreement? What happens with people who do not agree?

7. Decision makers determine the criteria for choosing external resources.

What issues will the new fix have to address? What will have to happen to make the solution congruent with group roles and company rules?

8. Designated decision makers search for possible solutions.

Since the decision makers will be involved in bringing the solution in and integrating it with the current setup, they must be part of the search. How will they determine which solutions will fit their criteria?

9. Locate potential solutions for decision makers to evaluate.

How will the group determine which solution is the answer? What will they need from the vendor to help with the decision?

How will they know when it's time to choose? *It is only when these questions are answered that a prospect is ready to buy.*

10. Purchase the resource.

Integrate it into the environment. Work to support the system while the new element is being integrated. Now the seller must support the buyer through service.

With the customary sales methodology, the buyer must go through this process internally, leaving potential external suppliers in a void. Between steps five and nine, the original decision maker becomes part of a decision-making team to research the solutions, frustrating many a seller when the Qualified Buyer, or QB, becomes QBs. Initially, the prospect has no reason to believe the system can't right itself internally, given that would be the most efficient solution. Even when it seems clear that a new piece of hardware is needed because of a reorganization, or new staff must be hired because of a consolidation, the first place people look for answers is on the inside.

When a buyer works with a buying facilitator, he is led through this process on the first call. He gets to see the problem and how it fits into the Problem Space, the possible solution and commensurate Solution Space. He gets to examine where internal resources will work and where they won't. Because the buyer's systemic issues are being addressed, there is nothing to object to. The buyer is being served in his decision-making process, and the only decision to be made is whether or not the product is the correct solution. And because it's all done through collaboration, the buyer can determine with the seller how they can continue working together.

The Buying Decision Funnel

The Buying Decision Funnel is a questioning technique that leads prospects through a sequential thinking process to assist them in collecting all the data needed to find the best available solution to their problem. Since much information stored in the brain is not

Present	Future
Where are you now? How did you get there?	Where are you going? How will you get there?
What's missing?	How did that happen?

Introduction of Team

How do you plan a fix with current resources?	At what point must you seek external resources?
What systemic issues must be satisfied?	What would you consider a solution?
What criteria will you use to choose an external solution?	What issues must be addressed when introducing an external solution?
How will you know when the system is ready for change?	How would you know if we meet your criteria for supplying the external solution?

Where do we go from here?

readily accessible, your questions will lead people to look in the appropriate areas in their brains to find answers. This is done in a linear fashion, with the questions becoming more and more specific. Ultimately you will uncover all of the issues, problems, decisions, environmental factors, and choices residing within the

culture that influence the problem and its solution. As Roger
Schank says in *The Creative Attitude*:

> Everything we hear about, see, or read gets stored in our
> memories. ...People have no sense that they are looking for a
> location in which to place (or find) a thought or
> experience... The place we choose for memory can serve to
> hide it forever if we have it labeled improperly, or to confuse
> it with other memories. (p. 14)

Later in the book he goes further:

> One must learn to be reminded in a way that provides a
> great deal more useful data which can help one to form
> valuable generalizations, test them out, fail, ask more
> questions, and thereby learn. (p. 98)

To continue to use the sock metaphor, you are moving from
the white sock drawer, to the colored sock drawer, and then to the
missing orange sock, and the criteria for solving the missing sock
problem.

As you can imagine, a prospect who knows he has a problem
and one who doesn't present two different circumstances for the
seller.

If the prospect is the initiator of the conversation, the seller
must work through what the prospect initially believes to be the
problem, usually arrived at without fully regarding the Problem
Space. Questions start with the presenting problem and move
sequentially through the decision-making stages we've just examined. As a seller, you must take into account the full complement
of cultural issues that present themselves, and carefully address
any differences between the prospect's initial determination and
the new information discovered while moving down the Funnel.

If the seller is the initiator of the conversation, the prospects
may not be aware they have a need or a problem. (This will be
the case regardless of whether the contact comes from a referral,
a phone book, or a qualified list.) Your job as the seller is to help
them down the Funnel. If the Funnel uncovers potential problem
areas not noticed previously, you may have a prospective buyer.
Of course, if their Present Situation gives them all they need, and

serves their Problem Space appropriately, there will be no need for a solution. In either case—a prospective buyer seeking a solution or a person unaware there is a problem of a missing orange sock— the Buying Decision Funnel will uncover any unresolved areas, including what is needed, how the need is to be met, and whether your product meets the criteria for solving the problem.

Moving from the Present Situation to the Desired Situation

People seek solutions when they want something different from what they've got—a different result, a different resource, a different response—or when what they've got isn't available in a timely fashion. In either case, they are not where they want to be. And since they can't get where they want to go unless they know where they are (have you ever tried to get directions when you didn't know your location?), they need to start with a comprehensive analysis of the Present Situation.

We'll begin our exploration of the Buying Decision Funnel by looking at its two major segments: the current state of affairs (the Present Situation) and the state that would exist if everything was as it should be (the Desired Situation). If everything in the environment is just as the prospect wants, then there is no need for him to look at anything different. If his insurance policies are up to date, if his finances are humming along, his Present Situation and his Desired Situation are the same and he has no need to be brought down the Funnel—even though you are selling the best insurance coverage, or the most successful estate planning package: **There's no sale without a buyer.**

Most people are basically comfortable in their current situation, even though they may say they're not, and would often rather stay where they are than experience the chaos of change. It is important, therefore, to begin your questions by examining all the components of the prospect's current environment (within the parameters of the product or service you are offering). This not only will put the two of you in rapport, but it will also help the prospect get a more complete view of all the components of the problem, and then lead him into the areas which helped create it.

The Desired Situation is what the environment would look like if everything were perfect. I am always really curious here: if people know what they want why haven't they achieved it already? Here is a major key to the puzzle: discover what has prevented the prospect from getting where he wants to be, and he may understand the factors involved in creating a solution.

As an example, let's look again at the problem in the customer service department which stemmed from the improperly handled company reorganization (chapter 6). The company's defined problem was unhappy customers. They wanted to upgrade their customer satisfaction. What was stopping them from having good customer satisfaction already? Once the buyer was brought down the Funnel, he would have had to notice the timing element: when customer satisfaction was good, when it stopped being good; how customer satisfaction was delivered when it was good, how it was being delivered now. Since the underlying values hadn't changed, what were the elements that had changed?

The more you can delve into the reasons prospects aren't where they want to be, the higher the probability that they can find the seed of the problem. A salesperson I recently trained told me of his frustration in getting a regular customer to place an order that had to be placed. When he asked the customer what was stopping him from getting the equipment, the customer replied that he thought it would only take two months for the order and set-up work to be completed and he wanted it to be on his next year's budget. The customer was then informed of the actual time the order and set-up would take, and the order was placed that day.

When people understand they are not where they want to be, they need a way to get to their Desired Situation. Once they know the underlying causes of their problems and they still don't make any changes, they either don't know how or don't want the situation to be different. It's your job to serve the prospect by facilitating the discovery of an answer here. If he doesn't know how to get where he's going and your product can help, bringing him down the Funnel will help him understand just how he can use your assistance. If he has no need to change his situation, the best thing to do is to end the relationship. One of the most difficult things for a seller to do is throw away a phone number.

I once had a prospect who claimed he needed my training, due to changes in his marketplace. But his top salespeople didn't want to change their way of selling—a clear case of the problem and Problem Space being disparate. His choices were to impose my way on them—and face the possibility of them quitting—or not get them trained. Guess who won? The fact that I noticed the need was immaterial.

How the Buying Decision Funnel works

I'd like to lead you through six industry-specific examples—a software product, a team-building program, a new brand of cereal, subscriptions to news magazines, political contributions, and insurance—to show you how the Buying Decision Funnel actually works. The questions that I'll be using are illustrations, and not necessarily the ones you might ask (Question formulation will be discussed in chapter 10). As I go along, I will highlight the reasons for the questions I've used to give you an idea of my direction and intent.

A word of caution before we begin: *Remember that the questions posed in the Buying Decision Funnel are not asked to give **you** information about the prospect, but to give the **prospect** the opportunity to sequentially access information in his brain that may not be readily available to him at the outset of your interaction.*

You begin, as always, with the prospect's current situation in regard to your product's area of expertise and follow the steps in the Funnel, which also follow the decision-making process.

Where are you now?
How did you get there?
It is vital to understand the decisions that went into the creation of a prospect's Present Situation. This will begin to give him an understanding of all the elements in the Problem Space and their relationship to each other. It's surprising how new all this available information seems to the prospect when he looks at it in

sequential fashion from a more objective place, which he'll get to through answering our questions.

Software: "We've been using software X and it has been working *pretty* well. We got it about *two years ago* when we had our last expansion."

Team building: "We've just done some management training around our vision. It was great! Our *people* have been *asking* for more integrated team approaches and they were real happy to have that training."

Cereal: "Boy, are there a lot of brands of cereal! We can only carry about fifteen brands with the space we've got. And the ones we've got are doing *pretty* well."

News magazines: "We read *mostly* home improvement magazines. We used to read lots more, but there just hasn't been time."

Political contribution: "We *don't really* contribute now that it's not tax deductible. We *used to give a lot.*"

Insurance: "We've got *just about* all the insurance we need. We got it all taken care of when my spouse turned fifty *a few years ago.*"

From the Present, you go to the Desired. Remember, if the prospect is exactly where he wants to be, there is no further conversation. I've highlighted the qualifiers in the above sentences to give you an understanding of how to think about what people may need. In the Cereal and Political Contribution responses, the prospects are pretty close to being fine with their Present Situation. There were enough qualifications, however, for me to ask one more question of them to make sure there is a Future to go to: *"You sound like you are doing fine where you are right now. Are there any conditions under which you would consider* (1) adding a new brand of natural cereal to your shelves? or (2) contributing to your local candidate even though you won't get a deduction?"

If the prospect answers "no" to this question, there is nowhere else to go. His Present Situation and Desired Situation are the same. But if he answers "yes," go forward.

**Where are you going? How do you plan on getting there?
What might be changing in the future?**

If a prospect is *not* where he wants to be, he has not found a
way of getting there yet or he would be there. That's where your
questioning skills come in.

> *Software:* "We're planning on hiring a few more people. I
> *think* our current system can handle a few more users."

> *Team building:* "We'd *consider more* training *if* we knew it
> would make our people as happy as the last training. It
> would have to be *consistent* with the last one, of course."

> *Cereal:* "We haven't considered adding any natural brands to
> our stocks *before*."

> *News magazines:* "Well, we haven't thought about adding any
> magazines. But there are *some* we've discontinued that *we
> miss*. I still don't think we'd have the time for more."

> *Political contribution:* "I know the school district *needs more*
> liberal-minded people. How's her campaign doing?"

> *Insurance:* "I *think* we're all set. *But* we haven't looked at the
> policy in some years. I think we're covered for everything
> we need. *Maybe* I should get that out and look at it again."

Notice how your questions are beginning to make the
prospects think in new ways. The next set of questions gets people to take a look at the Problem Space, separate from the problem itself.

**What's missing? How did that happen? What has stopped you
from getting where you want to be? How did that happen?**

Here the prospect will have to look at the decision-making
strategies he has used to date. Once he begins finding gaps in his
policy or thinking, he will need to go into less obvious parts of
his brain for answers. I'm combining Present and Desired here,
since so often prospects begin searching themselves as soon as they
notice something is missing.

> *Software:* "I *guess I need to find out* how many users our sys-
> tem can handle. *I'd better do that* this month since they'll be
> coming on board soon."

Team building: "We did that last program as our first foray into that type of training. Since it was a success, *I'm going to have to sit down* with the training group and team managers and *find out where we need to go.*"

Cereal: "My family eats the natural cereals—no sugar and whole wheat—but *I don't know how they would sell* in the store."

News magazines: "There are some events that I'm not caught up on since we've canceled our subscriptions to the major news magazines. *I'd just have to weigh* what's important right now."

Political contribution: "*I'd have to believe* that my contribution would help in some tangible way. It's important that the right people get elected."

Insurance: "*I guess I thought* we'd be covered adequately for at least a decade. *I'm not sure I know* why we wouldn't be, or if I need to do anything different. But that's a problem: I *should* know."

At this point in the Funnel, the prospect has begun to realize that he may not be where he should be. Because he may be discovering information that might have been stored in a mislabeled index, he might be getting confused.

Since most decisions involve more than one person, and it appears that the prospect might not be able to solve his problem with existing internal resources, the decision-making team is brought in.

Once a prospect realizes he needs an external resource most sellers jump in with: "Have I got a product for you!" "Obviously you'll need new software." "We run the best team building course." "Let me tell you how well our cereals do in supermarkets across the country." "Our service is different from anything on the market." In fact, when you attempt to push product at this point, the prospect defensively goes back to his original position because he may not know how to go further on his own and may be uncomfortable in unresolved territory.

If, however, you support the prospect in working through the discomfort and introduce questions about integrating his team or family members into the decision-making process, his process of discovery continues. In fact, the more you support discovery, the more you become part of the team.

Let's continue with the Funnel at the point the team or family or partner is introduced into the equation.

What do you have in place now that would solve your problem? At what point would you need more resources?

Because change is so unsettling, it is often shunned. The first thing people do when they notice that where they are is not necessarily where they want to be is to take a close look at the current environment to see if they can actually solve their problems with existing resources. Most sales approaches think this is the time to push or introduce product. It's not.

Software: "It *would be* great if our current software were adequate. *If* I find out it's *not,* I'll have to look at finding a way to upgrade our system. I'll need to have my systems person look into this for me. While he's at it, I'll have him see if there is anything else we need in the way of software to support our users."

Team building: "We don't have any internal training programs, but I think *it would be a good idea to ask* the previous trainers if they have other programs. Our people really liked them a lot."

Cereal: "We'd have to *make a policy decision* to add more natural products to our inventory if we were going to add your cereal. We haven't made that decision as yet."

News magazines: "I'd have to speak with my wife and see *if* she thinks she's *missing* some news. I know I don't always know what's going on out there, but I haven't wanted to bring in more magazines because we've seemed so happy without them. Maybe it's not about the magazines. Maybe we should just turn the TV on more often."

Political contribution: "I guess I'd feel better if I knew this candidate were sitting on the school board."

Insurance: "I think I'd better call my *current* agent and *find out what's going on.* My wife likes this guy and I think she'd be happier if he could add stuff to our policy."

Now that the prospects are discovering what would or wouldn't work with what they've got in place, the other aspects of the Problem Space start to make themselves known.

What's going on within the company/family that must be addressed or hasn't been looked at? What would you consider a solution?

Your questions are a great way to direct prospects toward uncovering all their issues.

Software: "We've been using this brand of software for a long time. In fact, the boss used to work for SBC company and knows most of the people who come out and take care of us. But it may be that we need some additional software. As a matter of fact, we're probably going to need some additional networking solutions."

Team building: "Our training manager brought this training group in. It was actually his idea. If the group doesn't do any other trainings I'd have to speak with him about whether he wanted to continue bringing in his own people or if he'd be willing to look at alternatives. I'd also want to talk with our employees to see what kind of follow-up they'd like."

Cereal: "Some of the people who shop in the store love the fact that they can get their old-time favorites here without having to deal with that new-fangled stuff: bran and yogurt. You know, the stuff those skinny people eat all the time. I guess if the shoppers wanted it I'd bring it in for them."

News magazines: "My wife and I need to figure out what's important in terms of our free time. I mean, if we're both feeling we need more news we'd have to decide if the TV or a magazine would be the best answer. First we'd have to fig-ure out if we need more news. I guess I'll have to sit down with her."

Political contribution: "I'd have to ask my husband if he'd mind contributing without a tax exemption. I'm sure he wouldn't, but we share a bank account. Also, I'd have to know where the funds were going before I'd consider giving money."

Insurance: "We've had our broker a long time. In fact, his son used to go out with our daughter—nice kid. For some reason I haven't called him lately. I'd feel better if he could handle any needs we've got. If I tell you what I've got, could you tell me if there is something I might be missing? I'd like for me and the wife to be fully covered. Maybe if there is something missing we could buy just that one thing from you."

Once people have begun to identify what needs to be addressed in their immediate environment—the Problem Space—they need to decide whether or not they have an internal solution and if that solution is broad enough to encompass the Problem Space. Then they need to understand how to choose the action to take.

What criteria will you use to choose an external solution? What will happen in your family or company if you decide to bring an unfamiliar element into the status quo?

These are difficult questions to answer, since people aren't usually cognizant of their values around any particular decision and can't decide on changes until they are. I often hear, "Boy, that's a good question." Prospects are experiencing some discomfort here, but it always amazes me what good sports they are in going in and finding their own answers. They are very appreciative that I've given them the opportunity to take a look at things in a new way and potentially open up new avenues for themselves.

Software: "It would have to be compatible with our current system. The boss would have to speak with you and see what you've got—if he hasn't already made a decision to bring his friend in and if our current supplier didn't have software that would handle it. Of course I don't know if we've even got all we need yet. If we decided to use software from your company, you'd have to get to know us here and we'd all have to feel comfortable enough with you to have you in for the training. I assume that training would come with any installation, am I right? Otherwise we wouldn't be interested. We do use this software as a team. Is doing an on-site demo part of your sales pitch? What exactly does your software do?"

Team building: "Before we'd bring a new program to our team it would have to be approved by our training manager. You'd also have to give us plenty of referrals. First, of course, we'd have to make sure our other supplier couldn't give us additional training. What did you say your training was about?"

Cereal: "We'd have to know you have a quality product. What's the name of the cereal again? I missed it the first time you told me. What are the ingredients? Have you sold it to many small grocery stores like ours? I'd love to see reports on small stores like mine. Also, the other employees would have to be in agreement to bring in the product and make the decision about bringing in this healthy stuff. Maybe we could do a shopper survey and leave it by the cash register. Do you have samples?"

News magazines: "As I said, my wife and I would have to decide what we're going to do with our time. What magazines do you have? Is there a trial period, or a short period we could subscribe for? We'd really need to try it out before making a commitment. We've gotten this one wrong before. Do you have money-back guarantees in case it doesn't work? I don't know, this might not be the right thing for us."

Political contribution: "If I knew where the money was going, and I thought my contribution would make a difference, I would consider contributing. I'd need to get agreement from my husband, and I'd need to decide how much I'm willing to give since it's not tax-deductible, and I'd have to think about it. Would you be willing to call me back?"

Insurance: "We'd have to be getting good service and you'd have to represent a reputable company. What types of insurance are you selling? How would I know you were reputable? I must be okay or my broker would have sold whatever it was to me. Could you tell me about the insurance for my grandchildren that you mentioned?"

We are deep into the Solution Space here. Prospects begin to ask themselves questions due to the confusion of being pushed out of their comfort zone. Note that these are not objections— there is nothing to object to. The prospects are needing information to make an informed decision. You must take care to answer only those questions they need answered to assist them in fully examining their options. *If you begin to tell them what you want them to hear, you will take them out of their own discovery.*

The next set of questions deals with the actual choice point. It's not enough to know that there is a problem, where it is, how it got there, and what needs to happen to fix it; the actual decision to do something different must occur.

> **How will you know when your environment is ready for a change? How will we know if the product I have meets your criteria for an external solution?**

These questions alone will move your sales cycle months forward. I cannot stress enough the first principle: **You have nothing to sell if there's no one to buy.**

Software: "If the boss can't get our needs met with our existing software supplier, I'd be glad to find out what you've got. Will you tell me how much your software costs? How many people does it serve? How easy is it to learn? Is it compatible with what we've got? Would you be willing to speak with our systems analyst to find out what else we need? I'd need some demos before we could make a decision, and all the users would have to vote on it. Can we manage that?"

Team building: "We're ready to do more training. It's a question of who will be doing it and when. Could you have a meeting with us and present your programs? Also let us know what kind of follow-up you do? You'd have to get team approval. Do you have some brochures I could hand out? I'd definitely need some referrals."

Cereal: "I think what I'll do is take a poll with customers and employees. If they want to expand, I'm willing to try your product as long as you come from a reputable company. But I'll only give it a three-month trial since I have so little shelf space. Deal?"

News magazines: "You'd have to call back after I've spoken with my wife. I really can't decide now, given what I've already said. I'd need to know a little about your company to make sure you aren't a fly-by-night operation, but you sound like a good guy. Can you send me something while me and the wife are deciding? Can you call me back next week at this time? I'll know by then."

Political contribution: "Let's talk next week. Can you get me the information I asked for by then? It's really important to me that I support the right people, so it's a balance of my finances and my values. I know the people you are working with, so I trust you. I just need to make a decision."

Insurance: "Can we spend some time finding out what I might need? How about coming to see me and my wife. If there's really something I need, I'd be willing to buy one policy from you, I guess. You seem to care about me. But I'd still want to check it out with my guy. Is next week okay?"

What you've done is explore the entire Problem and Solution Spaces with the prospect. Your questions have facilitated his ability to sequentially examine his needs and the needs of his company (team, family) and have brought him to discovery. You did not push product, manipulate a sale, use convincing strategies, create distrust, assume you had answers. You offered nothing but support to assist in discovering the best answers for his unique situation. In fact, the actual introduction of our product doesn't even appear until toward the end of the Funnel when *his* questions begin. At that point the Funnel actually reverses itself, with the buyer taking control by asking questions and the seller doing the talking. We'll address product presentation in chapter 12.

Of course, these scenarios are not real. I'm not certain I would want to sell to all of these people given the issues they have, especially the insurance scenario, and I certainly would want to speak with the systems analyst before moving further with the software scenario.

The process is a bit more complex than this, and I will be leading you through the pieces over the next several chapters, with the integration of the entire process in chapter 12. But you've now seen the skeleton of how to help someone discover what they need to buy. Indeed, you can move the sales cycle forward by *months* using this process, since you are bringing out issues that must be addressed at some point—and they are not usually addressed until much farther along.

SKILL SET #7:

The Buying Decision Funnel

Spend a day or two noting exactly how you go through the sales cycle currently. Notice the outcomes of your initial calls, and the goals and outcomes of your subsequent calls that lead to a close—or to a throwaway.

☐ What are the components of your first call with a new product to a prospect who is new to you? An existing client? Include:

How you build rapport;

How you build relationship with your opening;

How the prospect feels comfortable with you;

How information gets shared between you and the prospect;

The quality of shared information.

☐ How much do you know about the prospect's environment following the first call? About the Problem Space? About current available resources?

☐ At what point do you begin discussing the product?

☐ At what point does the prospect question you about the product?

☐ At what point do you begin to take over the call with your need to sell the product?

☐ How do you end the call?

Begin to use the questions in the Buying Decision Funnel.

☐ To practice getting all the information within the Problem Space, use the ten steps at the beginning of the chapter to jog your thinking. What skills do you need to formulate appropriate questions to help you through the ten-step process? What do you need to consider in order to think about the identifying problem versus the Problem Space?

☐ Notice difficulties you are having with your old patterns of being the one in charge of content, wanting to sell, and pitching. Stand up or sit back in your chair to gain perspective. Look down at yourself from the ceiling. At what point do you notice discomfort with the Buying Decision Funnel? What skills do you use when you are uncomfortable?

☐ Notice differences in responses and in the quality of information you are receiving.

☐ What skills do you have that enable you to put aside your need to sell and support a prospect's discovery through the ten steps outlined at the beginning of this chapter?

☐ Notice difficulties you may be having with question formulation. What skills do you need in order to use the Buying Decision Funnel easily? Make sure you are using the mental filter of seeing yourself as a servant, rather than a seller.

☐ Keep looking down at yourself from the ceiling. Do you see a servant or a seller? How do you know the difference? What do you need to change? How will you do that? How are you being perceived by the prospect? How do you know?

Within a month or so of practice, you will have the Buying Decision Funnel at a level of conscious competence. It will take another month before it becomes totally natural. Remember that you've had years of conditioning to pitch and take control of the conversation by having all the answers.

Also remember that you are promoting discovery. A prospect always buys what he needs when it's the right time, the right product, and he's in a relationship with plenty of rapport.

Chapter 8

Creating a Relationship of Trust and Collaboration

When our job was to sell product, we were responsible for meeting our quotas, for professional demeanor and skills, for honest representation of our company and product. Now, with Buying Facilitation, we have an additional level of responsibility: we must take responsibility for the way our communication with the prospect proceeds.

That means it is your job to create an environment where you understand and are understood, to create a communication that works to serve both seller and prospect. *It is not okay for your prospective buyers or clients to be "jerks" just because they won't buy or because they don't understand you.* They often don't know you well enough to make a great effort and can't be blamed.

In Buying Facilitation, it is the seller's responsibility to create comfort, rapport, understanding, discovery, and collaboration when picking up that phone for the first time, or when walking into an office. Without those qualities, there's no sale anyway.

If you think about what happens when you close a sale easily, you will find you've had an almost special relationship with that person from the beginning. It just flows. It's different from the others. It took little effort. You were in the middle of a relationship from the moment you met. There were few barriers.

My guess is that you stumbled upon a person who buys the way you sell, who communicates in a similar fashion to you, and/or who speaks in a similar fashion with similar language and voice patterns. You can learn to do all that on purpose, which allows you to enter into each call with the same chance of comfort and rapport. Again, the only reason a prospect should not become a client is because she doesn't need the product. Remember: **People buy using their own buying patterns.**

This chapter will present different ways to take the responsibility this new job as servant requires. The first is to create a "We Space."

The "We Space"

While a "We Space" is natural in a marriage or friendship, it has not been a natural mode of relating in the sales process. Think about a conversation you have had recently with a friend. Now think about one with a prospect. How are they different? And why?

We often make our sales calls—the initial ones at least, until we form a relationship with a prospect-turned-client—from the task mode. Our voices sound distant: we're speaking like officious people who are obviously important and good at our jobs. We're professionals, and we make sure the person on the other end of the communication realizes that through our voices, which have little intimacy.

A new client of mine, Jane, was a very busy partner in an insurance firm. She wanted me to teach her Buying Facilitation in person, outside of a classroom setting. I spent an hour with her going through the principles and beliefs as best I could, made a few calls on her behalf so she could hear what the process sounded like, and then handed the phone over to her to try it herself when she felt ready.

She dialed a number, a person answered, and my client sat there with her mouth ajar in stunned silence. She didn't know what to do.

From the other end of the phone came silence. Then I heard, "Hello?... Hello?... Hellllloooo!... Hello, hello, hello. Is anyone there?"

Jane burst out laughing. So did the other person.

"Ah, so there *is* someone on the other end of the phone. Would you like to start speaking yet?"

There was no way Jane could go into "important person" since she had already blown it. By the time she finally opened her mouth, she had begun a "We Space."

"I'm really here. I am learning a new sales technique and I just lost it. I'm surprised you hung in with me."

Jane opened a six-figure account with this person on their second meeting.

From One Human Being to Another

It's not always this easy, of course, but when one human being talks to another there's usually warmth, acceptance, understanding, and allowance for error. It is when the machines get talking to each other that there is no room for mistakes: **Relationship comes first, task second.**

The classical definition of a communication is an interaction having both a sender and a receiver. As we've seen, the Traditional sales method of "open, pitch, present, close" presupposes only one side of the equation—the seller's side—and creates objections and rejection.

In *Sales on the Line,* I characterize a "We Space" as a unique system between two people who meld and modify their individual needs to act and make decisions through the relationship. In other words, the interaction between the two people is unique to them and *because of* this relationship, new thinking, new actions, new possibilities occur. Below is an illustration of "We Space."

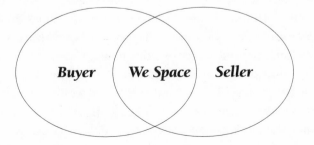

By making a people connection, by bringing your personality into your communication, by setting up a collaboration in which two people are able to speak the truth (like announcing it's a sales call), by taking the responsibility to create a comfortable environment between you, by having an agenda to serve, you engender trust.

In reality, the only way a prospect will consider getting needs met through a particular supplier is if there is rapport and shared values. And as discussed earlier, the prospect is unlikely to take the initial responsibility to create this.

I hired a new saleswoman and she was having a very difficult time getting rid of her old persuasion tactics. She'd start off fine, get halfway down the Funnel, lose her ability to ask the right questions, and then stop, knowing it was better to stop speaking than use her old patterns. She'd call me, annoyed with herself for having lost it, for not doing the method "right." She was so lost in the learning curve that a few prospects actually said things to her like the following:

"Tell me where you are going with this."

"I'm lost. What's the point here?"

"What exactly are you trying to get at?"

"This sounds interesting but I don't fully understand what you're trying to say."

The prospects were staying with her while she floundered, and actually helping her through her confusion. And these were cold telesales calls with no prior contact. The reason why they stayed with her and actually helped her along was because she was *being* with them rather than trying to get them to buy. She was trying to help them help themselves, and while the method was being *done* ineffectively, her ability to be a person, to be human and vulnerable, to make mistakes and be honest, got her business with three out of the four prospects above. Their companies, by the way, were all multinational Fortune 500 companies, and the people who were helping her out were the sales managers.

My saleswoman couldn't figure out why these sales managers weren't hanging up on her and why they would consider doing business with her when she didn't get it "right." *It's not about right, it's about relationship—the being not the doing.* It's about the seller meeting the prospect through a relationship instead of through a job. It's about the seller giving up an officious voice and just *being* with the prospect—person to person. This creates trust. This is how sales increase. Even the Buying Facilitation methodology is secondary to putting people first, as we've seen in the example with Jane.

How to Do "We"

Forming a "We Space" with a stranger is a business skill few of us were taught. You must align yourself with the buyer's values and culture. You must have a shared perception of the problem, Problem Space, solution, and Solution Space. While this is done predominantly through questioning and listening skills (which I offer in the next few chapters), you must begin by being in rapport and getting rid of your need to sell. *People buy using their own buying patterns, not a seller's selling patterns. The buyer has the answers. Relationship comes first.*

I recently got one of those annoying telemarketing calls at nine o'clock in the evening.

> "Hi. Is Mr. or Mrs. Morgen there please?"
> "Is this a sales call?"
> "What's the matter, you don't like be addressed as Mrs.?"
> "What can I do for you?" I was getting curious here. I couldn't wait to hear how she'd handle this.
> "My name is Joanne Smith. I'm calling from TeleWorld Communications and I've got a special I'd like to tell you about in terms of your long-distance coverage."
> "I'm using XYZ now, and I'm really happy with them. They are giving me everything I need."
> "Do you know how much money you are wasting by being with them? Let me show you . . ."
> "Money is not my criterion. I'm getting good service, and I'm happy to pay for it."
> "You're not even giving me a chance to tell you about my product. I'm assuming you are a smart consumer."

"Are you telling me I'm stupid if I don't buy?"

"Whoops. I guess I blew this one, didn't I?"

This call really happened.

There was obviously no "We Space," no desire to serve, no belief that I had my own answers, no relationship, no respect, and no buyer. Imagine if she'd started out with rapport, a "We Space," and the desire to serve. It might have gone like this:

"Hello. My name is Joanne Smith from TeleWorld Communications. Who am I speaking with please? . . . And if this is too late for you, let me know because this is a sales call."

"It is late. What are you selling?"

"TeleWorld is a long-distance carrier. And I'll make it short because it's so late. What are you doing about working with a long-distance carrier?"

"I'm using XYZ company and I love them."

"That's nice to hear. I rarely hear anyone speak well of their carrier. It sounds like you're all set. Are there any conditions under which you would consider exploring an alternate carrier?"

"What I love about XYZ is their service. I suppose if another carrier would give me the exact same service and save me money, I'd consider it. But I'd have to be sure I'd be getting the same service."

"What I hear is that service is your priority and that saving money is secondary. How would you know if we could offer at least the same service you are getting now?"

"I'd need references from folks who have been with you for over one year. But I need you to know that I'm really happy with my current carrier and probably won't switch."

"I hear that. Would you rather end the conversation now?"

"I'm happy to call a few references and make up my mind then. But don't hold out much hope. I'll give you a shot, so get me some names."

Notice the difference between the calls: in the first, the seller was taking care of her own needs; in the second, we were in sync, which the seller created by taking my needs into consideration and genuinely caring about my time and my loyalty. I offered to look at her product, not because of her need but because there was a possibility that it might serve me. There was collaboration and respect. This is "We Space." She entered into this space with me, in fact created it, by taking direction from me and my stated needs.

The more help you can give your prospects in their decision making, the sooner you can work together—or not. Please use this Skill Set to practice creating a "We Space" for forming collaborative environments.

SKILL SET #8:

Creating a "We Space"

Name the specifics of how you relate with friends and family during a few interactions. Include: comfort, rapport, respect, types of information exchanged, dialogue flow. Notice the differences in different types of interactions. Also notice the similarities.

☐ What skills and behaviors make up the comfort zone you are in? Note specifically the skills you inherently use to do your part toward creating this. Some areas you might want to notice include:

Entering the conversation and leaving: How do you do that? What do you do with your voice? Your tone, tempo, volume?

Your intent: Do you want to listen? Be heard? When do those needs shift? As a result of what is said to you? As a result of your needs when you entered the interchange?

Your body language: At what point do your gestures or postures shift?

Your language patterns: How do you choose your words? Your silences?

Your unconscious behaviors: What do you notice you do during the interaction that you were previously unaware of? What do you do consistently in each interaction? What do you do sometimes? How do you know to do something different? Or the same?

☐ What are the skills you consistently use in every interaction in which there is comfort and respect? What changes occur in you when you are no longer comfortable?

Name the specifics of how you relate with colleagues and business contacts.

☐ Notice any differences from interactions with family and friends. Notice similarities.

☐ Notice what interactions come easily. Which are more difficult? Why?

☐ What communication behaviors do you exhibit that you have chosen consciously with specific people? What did you have to do with your brain to create conscious choice?

☐ What do you do when your communication patterns are ineffective? How do you alter an ineffective exchange while it is happening? What could you have done differently at the time? What skills do you have in place to choose differently?

Bring this new awareness to your sales calls, both telephone and face-to-face.

☐ Notice how you are *being* with clients versus prospects.

☐ Notice the differences in your communication while being with someone with whom you have an established relationship versus while being with a stranger.

☐ Notice the differences in your communication styles in different prospect situations. What makes them different? Or the same? What makes them effective? Or ineffective?

☐ How do you go about choosing your communication behaviors in a work situation versus a personal exchange?

☐ What skills do you need to add to your work interactions that you currently use exclusively in your personal interactions? What are the differences in your communication skill levels in established relationships versus prospect relationships?

☐ What skills do you need in order to use any of your current, effective communication skills in any interchange, regardless of who your communication partner is?

How to Avoid Using Selling Patterns

When you use a particular approach to sell, you play a numbers game. *When you have even one selling pattern, you will only be able to sell to those people who buy the way you sell. All those people who need your product and are uncomfortable with the way you sell will not buy from you.* You are cutting out at least two-thirds of all the prospects who are potential buyers *because your selling patterns are out of rapport with their buying patterns.*

How can a seller with a pitch and a need to push product ever learn to serve another and support full collaboration?

One evening I got a call from a woman whose voice sounded intimate, as if we were long-standing friends—except I didn't recognize her voice.

"Hi!"

"Hi. Who's this?"

"Sue Laguna from Xstar. You called for information about six months ago and I'm just getting back to you. Sorry it took so long."

"I did? What type of information?"

"About one of our software products, so I thought I'd let you know about our whole range so you could see which one you wanted."

"What did I call about? I don't remember doing that."

"Well, it was a while ago, and you might not remember. So while we're on the phone, why don't I just tell you about our product line . . ."

"Excuse me. Will you please tell me what specifically I called about? Or are you lying to me to get your foot in the door?"

She hung up. She could have called me and said:

"Hi. My name is Sue Laguna from Xstar and we're a software application firm. Is this a good time to speak? It's a sales call."

I buy application software all the time. I would have loved to have spoken with her. I just didn't like being lied to and manipulated. I didn't like being a number rather than a person. She was putting her product and her need to sell ahead of consideration for me. By doing that, she lost a sale.

My Seller's Ego Needs to Sell

When I hear my "seller's ego" being disdainful and preparing for battle with the "jerks" who aren't "getting it," I use that too-familiar internal dialogue as an alarm that my selling patterns want to come out and play and that my ego is off and running. I say to myself, "Ahem . . . excuse me?? What's going on here?" as a reminder that I have a new choice: that it's my job to serve, not sell, that I don't need to be right, I need to be in relationship. Operating from the belief that my job is to serve, I have a good start on getting out of my selling patterns.

I hear from people who are using Buying Facilitation what a relief it is to not have all the answers, to not have to be the expert. When they were using the older sales approaches, they went into fight-or-flight, win-or-lose, right-or-wrong in each interaction. It took an enormous emotional toll on them: their identities were caught up in being experts and performing. They believed that if they didn't get it right, they wouldn't make the sale. With Buying Facilitation, their identity is no longer caught up in being an expert. They don't need to be right, just to collaborate and "figure it out" with their communication partner.

I have also experienced that within the first five to ten minutes of a sales call there's a good indication of whether or not there's a business and product fit. When the questions in the Buying Decision Funnel bring out that the prospect is happy with her current situation, that she is satisfied with the answers she has found, that there are no conditions under which she would make any changes, the seller must trust that there is nowhere else to go and move on. Remember: **You have nothing to sell if there's no one to buy,** and you are **promoting discovery not product.**

To be honest, it's scary the first few days you try this, since you are not using your old selling habits. As we will see in chapter 12, there is no opening gambit—although there is rapport building; no close—although products get purchased; no pitch—although products get discussed; no objection handling or rejections because there is no adversarial relationship. We are using *no selling patterns*, but your sales will increase astronomically. And your values will be congruent, both at home and in the workplace.

SKILL SET #9:

Selling Patterns versus Buying Patterns

☐ Note the behaviors you use when you sell, for example:

How you open the call;

How you pitch or enter the call;

How you get the prospect/client talking;

How you answer questions;

How you position your product;

How you deal with objections;

The type of objections you get; and

How you close.

☐ What happens when you consider not using selling patterns? What is your understanding of how you will approach the prospect? Your job?

☐ What issues come to mind when you consider being in service rather than having a job selling?

☐ What is your thinking on how you will close sales or meet quotas without using selling patterns?

☐ Are you clear about the differences between selling and supporting someone's buying decisions? If not, reread this chapter.

☐ What do you currently do to offer support to your prospects? What are the results?

☐ Do any discomforts come up when you think of altering your sales approach? What are they? How would you know if/when you would be willing to attempt it? Under what conditions? How would you know if it had been worth it? Under what conditions would you try it again?

☐ What do you need from this book to support your discovery of how you can facilitate buying rather than selling? What do you need from yourself? What type of support do you need from outside—your team, your colleagues, other books, personal decisions?

Supporting an Informed Decision

As part of the decision-making process and the collaboration between buyer and seller, the seller has the responsibility to support solution finding, with the seller's product only one of the potential solutions. Indeed, this is what Buying Facilitation is all about: serving the prospect to find the most appropriate solution.

Since you're helping with the discovery of a solution, one of the controversial suggestions I offer is that you be fully aware of all your competition and actually make available whatever information buyers need in order to make an informed decision—to bring all the necessary facts back to the decision-making body. *The decision makers are going to do this anyway.* It's no secret there are other products that do what your product does. You might as well offer up all the competitor's information and save weeks in the sales cycle. I don't do this on many calls. But on ones where they state they are "early into the information-gathering cycle" or "just beginning to do our homework" or "looking at all of the options," I give them a hand.

I ask my prospects how far along they are in their research. I then summarize all the elements I know to be vital to their purchase. When I get agreement that I'm understanding their situation correctly, I tell them I have information on the competition and am happy to go through all of the other products in line with their criteria if they'd like. When there is a product that is similar to mine in many ways, I point that out:

"Product X is similar. It does many of the things ours does with some differences. It can give you X, Y, Z. It does L, M, N that ours doesn't do. It will not give you A or B and you would have to decide how important that is to you. And the price compares . . ."

Your prospects aren't fools. They will come up with the same information. For me, putting all this out in a first or second call makes my job more efficient, as well as more service-oriented. The issues have to be dealt with. If they're not, the sales cycle gets longer, if nothing else. Personally, I would rather know if a prospect would choose to pay less for an inferior product because price is such a highly valued criterion. Or if the head decision maker used to work for one of the competition and has friends there. Or if several people on the team have tried an earlier iteration of my product and found it difficult to use. When I have this information, I can go back and ask questions to help people discover what they need from me to move forward. I would much rather know my price is too high, or my product or company not respected, on a first call.

One of the rewards of bringing all of this information to light is an increased trust of your intent to serve. This collaboration will also help put you onto the decision-making team. That doesn't mean they will necessarily buy your product. But you will have served them, and they will give you references and probably use you and your product in the future. I notice I have a very active "dead" file.

You also save so much time by doing this that it pays for itself in the end. You save time on all those lost-in-space follow-up calls. You save time because you are not working with a prospect for months before they decide to go with another product. You save time by moving the sales cycle forward.

By putting relationship first, by taking the responsibility to create a collaboration, by supporting your prospect's buying patterns, you will be in a position to be trusted and respected. Now you must learn how to serve your prospect by getting her to discern exactly what she needs and how she needs it.

Chapter 9

Supporting the Process of Discovery

By this point, I am sure you are realizing the enormity of the shift I am suggesting in the job of sales. You might be asking yourself, "How do I approach a sales call, earn a living, have a product purchased—all without selling? How do I facilitate a buying environment to make certain my product finds the right home at the right price? How do I maintain my ethics and get my products sold?"

You do, after all, have quotas and your companies need to sell their products to exist.

Earning a Living with Ethics

First of all, you need to actually *believe* that it is your job to serve, to facilitate discovery, to have questions instead of answers. But this seems to go against the reasons you went into sales: the very basis of sales has been the development of strategies in every facet of the sales cycle to give you control.

One reason people go into sales is because their personality traits fit into the skill set of that profession. It is rare to find sellers who are shy, not confident, nonverbal, impersonal, lazy, introverted, unable to make a quick decision, distasteful of activity or socializing, or unwilling to help others. Sellers are a charming lot, exuding confidence, taking charge and getting things done, and working whatever hours it takes to accomplish a goal. Most sellers I've met take pride in their willingness and ability to help others.

In fact, getting rid of your ego, your need to win and be right, your need for control—the very attributes sales people are humorously known for—is the hardest part of Buying Facilitation. I can say this from personal experience, because I sometimes miss the rush I used to get when I could really go in and make a difference using my charm and personality and brains. But those very attributes gave me a need to control situations that in my everyday life wouldn't be mine alone to control. In fact, when I ask sellers if they treat their friends the way they treat prospects and buyers, they respond, "No way."

In Buying Facilitation, you use your great repertoire of skills to support the needs of others, rather than your own need for the spotlight. (For me, that's what I really wanted to do anyway.) Make no mistake, however, there is a lot of control in Buying Facilitation—it is just a different kind of control. It is a control that gives the prospect the ability to sequentially order his thinking to find his own answers. With Buying Facilitation, you can be congruent with your own values while serving your clients; you can treat your prospects and buyers as you would friends and family; and you can make money.

Once you have created a "We Space," and are on the same side of the table with your prospect, looking at the same goals, you must fully understand the issues involved in what *causes* a prospect to buy something. You also need to take responsibility to create an *environment of discovery* and use skills that support a prospect's *decision to buy*.

Facilitating a Buying Environment

Your job is to facilitate discovery, to help people figure out how they can best get their needs met, either alone, if it's a singular decision, or with their team, if it's a larger or corporate sale. If you can form a "We Space" and create a collaboration on the first call, and use the questions in the Buying Decision Funnel to facilitate discovery, there really is no reason why you can't become part of the decision-making team from the beginning—even if selling your product is not the ultimate outcome. If you are not able to form some type of a collaboration in which both you and your prospect decide together how to move forward, you will be left in a "seller's void" while the decision-makers work on their own—without you. That's what's happening each time you hear "We'll call you back when we're ready" or "Call back next week." *There's no sale without a buyer. People buy only when they can't fill their own needs.*

In other words, you can help shorten the decision-making process. It's one of the ways you can serve your customers. Let me share with you an example of what can happen when this process is short-circuited.

I got a funny call one day from a man in a car.

"I was just driving to an appointment listening to a tape of yours that someone gave me. It's great. We need you to come in and help us. Can you send me materials? Answer some quick questions? I'll call you from my office next week and we can spend some time talking."

I sent him my materials and called him the next week. He didn't return my call. A month later, I got a call from one of his people, stating her boss had told her to call and ask me about available training. She was excited. She was ready to sign up. She never called me back.

My salesperson took over the account and called the boss a month later. They were going through a reorganization, didn't know what job descriptions were even necessary, and obviously wouldn't know what kind of training they'd need until after the reorganization was completed. Since he'd originally called me from a car phone, I did not ask him any questions to support his transition, so not only was I in the dark, but his process took longer than it would have if I'd had the chance to facilitate his thinking. During the wait between calls, the saleswoman in me decided that I'd said something wrong on the call, that here again were prospects that couldn't make up their minds, that they were calling lots of sales trainers to get the best deal. . . . I had no way of knowing the reality because I was out of the loop.

This sales process took four months from initial contact to closed sale. It might have taken half that time if I'd had the chance to support his discovery.

The point is the level of responsibility you take to support the prospect's discovery. The sooner in the process you are able to use your skills to do that, the sooner both you and your prospect will recognize whether or not your product fits. As the seller, you will need to take initial responsibility for creating the search. We will discuss the skills you will need for this over the next few chapters. For now, just recognize that the prospect has no reason, initially, to trust your intent. If your intent is not grounded in the desire to serve with the skills of collaboration, *you may be met with resistance and vague answers, if not a longer sales cycle.* Prospects quickly know the difference between being manipulated and being served.

I'd like to introduce another skill to help guide your interaction and move the conversation to where it will benefit discovery.

Structure versus Content: A Different Type of Control

Imagine you are going white-water rafting. You and your partner are both preparing for the trip. You are responsible for all the gear, such as the life jackets and the emergency supplies—the content, the details, if you will. Your partner is making sure the boat is safe

and actually takes a course on navigating through rough waters—
he is responsible for the structure, the container in which everything else resides. Who has the most control over the safety of the
trip?

In sales, information, details, the story of your product is the
content of your communication, much like the emergency gear in
the boat. Your prospect's content is their story—filled with facts,
conjectures, opinions, needs, feelings. Stories are dynamic and rich
in subjective description.

The direction the communication takes and what it covers is
guided by the structure, that holds and contains the details of the
story. The structure is the framework, the container, the struts—
the boat. The structure is like a newspaper headline that encapsu-
lates the story, or an ice cream cone when it holds the ice cream.
The container is lean, static, dispassionate, and relatively objective.

Use the structure of the Buying Decision Funnel—the direction, type, and timing of the questions—as the means to contain
the conversation within those areas where you can serve the
prospect. In other words, the Buying Decision Funnel becomes the
structure you work within. It leaves out any information extrane-
ous to the prospect's discovery. Through the structure, you can
keep a tight reign on the direction and content of the conversation, limiting it to discussions about office supplies when your
product is office supplies and curbing discussions about how the
stingy CFO stopped buying sodas to put in the company fridge.

Therefore, during the discovery part of the interaction, you
can take control of the structure of the conversation and the
prospect is in control of the content—win-win. (See the illustration on next page.) This gives the prospect support to search
throughout the Problem Space for the full spectrum of issues to
be examined. While it might seem that the prospect has examined
that arena a myriad of times before you met him, it's a rare interaction in which the Funnel questions don't find some crucial piece
of the Problem Space that has not been taken into account. The
prospect is usually too close to the situation to get perspective,
and your questions move him away from the subjective details,
into a more objective view.

Timing is important in introducing the details—content—of your product. When a prospect has not gone through the full discovery process and is not fully aware of the specifics he must go through to find and install his ultimate solution, discussion of your product is moot. Once the prospect has determined his solution, and your questions have led him to specificity, he's eager to know the details of your product. Again, you're only asking questions in your area of expertise, so the prospect will have some idea of what you're selling. Do you remember the office supplies example in chapter 4? The seller's questions enabled the office manager to specify the tasks and time involved in refurbishing the shelves herself, which sparked her interest in how she might use her time differently.

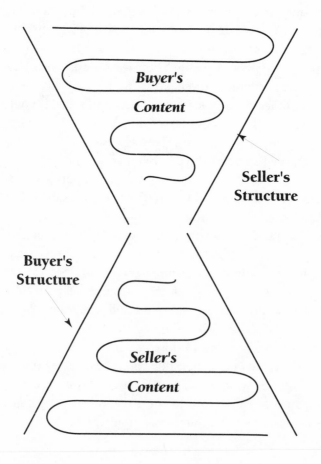

Using Your Pitch

Once a prospect understands that there is in fact a need, and can name the criteria he and the decision-makers will use to choose an external resource, he'll want some concrete information from you. Here the process will reverse itself, with you being in content while speaking about your product—your pitch, if you will—and the prospect being in structure through his questions— win-win. Here you can answer your prospect's questions, offer details about your product, discuss 'specials'—it's your turn. Just make sure you address only the areas of interest for the prospect, and don't use this as an excuse to say all the things you may want to say that might be irrelevant.

Moving between the structure of discovery questions and the content of a pitch is an interesting balance; it takes practice. Let's examine this further.

In the old sales paradigms, open questions were used to get the prospect to give us information in order to direct our pitch. But before the Solution Space is fully depicted, information relative to your product is irrelevant. Having a solution to the problem isn't enough.

In the new sales methodology, staying within the structure of the Buying Decision Funnel helps you to listen by keeping you out of details you don't need to know and giving you perspective on the Problem and Solution Spaces. You will need this stark level of understanding to help direct the prospect down the Funnel, toward his own answers. **The buyer has the answers; the seller has the questions.**

In fact, the person speaking about content, discussing details and distinctions, is not able to direct the interaction. Simply put, *the person in content is out of control of the direction the interaction takes.*

Salespeople have spent years learning the specifics of the content of their product, and then wonder why, after positioning the product brilliantly, addressing the needs they've uncovered, getting agreement that their product's features and functions would benefit the prospect, they are out of control in the conversation. It is because the prospect knows the seller is serving himself. He knows he is not being served. When this happens, the prospect takes control over the structure of the call *which the seller has given him* and calls the shots: says he's busy, not interested, has no money; doesn't return calls, wants proposals, wants information to be sent. But when you collaborate and share control and trust, you make decisions together, and they are better decisions as a result. You are, in fact, sharing the control of the interaction. Win–win.

I once went into content too early in a call and ended up giving a monologue before the prospect knew what he was listening for. I finally stopped and said, "Is there anything you need?" The prospect said, "You've been speaking nonstop for four minutes and thirty-two seconds; I don't need to waste any more of my time," and he hung up.

When you are speaking at the content level too early in the conversation, you can have no earthly idea what your prospect needs, what you should be addressing, or how he needs to hear it. The prospect is still in the white sock drawer and has no place to put the information you are offering. When you get into your content, the prospect distrusts that you have his needs in mind. And he's right—you don't.

SKILL SET #10:

Structure and Content

Think of a recent prospecting conversation. Remember the communication as much as possible.

☐ How did you lead the conversation? What parts did you take control of? How did you create and maintain the direction of the conversation?

☐ Did you lose control of the conversation at any point? How did that occur?

☐ What would need to happen differently for you to maintain control of the direction of the conversation?

- ☐ If you maintained control of the conversation throughout, what skills did you use to do that? What were the consequences? Did both you and your prospect get your needs met? Did the outcome take into account the entire Problem Space?

- ☐ Was there a collaboration? How did that occur? What specific skills did you use?

- ☐ What skills would you need in order to maintain better control of the direction of the call?

Staying Objective: *Observer* versus *Self*

One of the easiest ways to stay in structure is to remain objective. Since you are selling a product and have so much content knowledge about the product, it's difficult to control the desire to go in at the first sign of need and shout "I've got just the thing for you!"

Seeing the Problem from *Observer*

There is a skill you can use to keep you "in choice" (able to choose your communication behaviors in the conversation) so that you can assume the responsibility to support your prospect. It is a way to remain objective while bringing the prospect through the Buying Decision Funnel. I call it being in *Observer.* Unless you are outside of yourself, you are unable to notice something occurring that needs a different behavior from the one you are exhibiting.

You need to be in a witness position (Observer) in order to see both your prospect and yourself while leading the prospect through the decision-making process, but still keeping your product knowledge and expertise available to use.

Observer will find you hovering over the interaction to determine what choices you need to make next to offer your support.

From your removed vantage point, you can formulate questions and offer summaries of what was said based on the prospect's need to know rather than your need to sell. By standing neutrally outside the Problem Space, you can help the prospect scan the parameters of the space and define and broaden the area, often on the first call.

Again, go back to the office supplies example. The office manager wasn't aware of the additional time commitments she was placing on herself unnecessarily, nor the potential inefficiency of her operating procedures. In the customer service story in chapter 6, the director of customer service thought there was a problem with the way the people were executing customer service procedures and missed the human issues.

As I've discussed earlier, I believe it is our responsibility to our prospects to assist their discovery. Having the choice to move into the Observer position with your expertise helps you to serve. It is from this position that you can make decisions; you will have a clear view of the best way to use your expertise responsibly.

Operating Out of *Self*

When you are operating out of your own needs, from your own content, you are in *Self*. When you are in Self, you are in your ego and not collaborating. Self has a hard time facilitating a prospect's process of finding different answers from the ones you'd like him to have. Self wants to "create a need," or pitch, or manipulate the questions around to what you want the prospect to know about your product. Self is the personality doll that operates on automatic, so you don't have a neutral choice of communication approaches when operating from Self

This Self, a delightful professional, cannot get perspective on the total situation. In fact, the prospect is often in Self during the time he is in content, explaining his environment. This fact alone will keep him from seeing all possible solutions.

Self holds your personalities, your charm, and is just as important as Observer. But because you are distant and disinterested when you speak from Observer, you must *speak* from Self. You must learn how to *decide*—to ask questions, agree, or summa-rize—from Observer, and *deliver* the communication from Self.

In order to be able to serve your prospect by helping him see his whole Problem Space and recognize his choice points, *and* deliver your questions and summaries in a way that brings your uniqueness and expertise to the interaction, you must be able to move fluidly between Self and Observer.

Please use this next skill set as a practice session for learning to use Observer and Self with conscious choice.

SKILL SET #11:

Moving between *Self* and *Observer*

In your mind's eye, imagine or remember yourself having dinner with one other person. Take a moment to get a good look at the mental image.

☐ How many people do you see sitting at the table: one or two?

If you see one—your dinner companion—you are in Self.

If you see two—both your dinner companion and yourself—you are in Observer, since you must be removed from the table, possibly somewhere on the ceiling, in order to have the perspective to see yourself in the picture.

In order to see the whole picture *and* be in a trusting relationship—a "We Space"—you need the flexibility to move back and forth between Self and Observer.

☐ Practice this skill daily with your friends and family. Notice yourself engaged in conversation, excited, annoyed—just being you.

Then, in your mind's eye, step back and move to the ceiling and be in Observer. Watch yourself interacting. Notice yourself, your movements, your sphere of influence, how people react to you.

Then move back into Self. Experience your normal feelings and movements. Feel the differences between the two positions.

☐ Notice the differences in the feelings in your body, level of mental engagement, your viewpoint, the way you relate, your ability to have a grasp of the machinations of the interactions.

☐ Notice any difficulties in moving back and forth between the two positions.

☐ Where are you most comfortable? Where do you usually reside? From which position do you have the greatest number of behavioral choices if you were to notice the need to do something different?

☐ Notice how involved you are at a personal level while in the Self position.

☐ Notice how much more of the situation you can see from the Observer vantage point. Notice the curiosity rather than judgment. Notice your psychological distance from your need to be product-based.

☐ Practice this shifting for several days. Then bring it into your sales calls. Begin to notice where you reside while you are selling. If you spend most of your time in Self, what is the effect of this on your interactions? How different is it when you move to Observer? What is the difference between relating from Observer and relating from Self?

Decide from Observer; deliver from Self.

☐ Notice the flexibility and the ability to see a broad range of issues that you have in Observer. Notice the genuineness and the humanness that you have in Self. Notice you don't have answers from Observer—only questions.

In order to maintain the Observer position, sit well back in your chair or stand up.

I have trained thousands of people in this methodology and have discovered that when people are in Self they are hunched forward and tense in their upper bodies. When they are in Observer, they are sitting back or standing up or at least loose in their upper bodies. I don't know why it works to change physiology—but it does.

☐ Notice at what point in a communication you move forward.
That's the point at which you lose your objectivity and need to
get back into choice. You can do this easily by leaning back. For
some reason, physiology and mental patterns work together to
put you right back into Observer. Try it.

How to Use Buying Patterns in the Funnel

You can support a prospect's discovery by working with his buying patterns. This keeps you in rapport and maintains trust. Buying patterns are unique to each group or individual. I've received calls from strangers interested in my training who say, "I've read your book. When can you come train us?" Others ask me for lists of referrals even after we've collaborated to discover solutions. Some prospects need face-to-face visits. Some do all their interviewing on the phone. Other people let their team member make the final decisions.

Every single sales situation is unique. I certainly wish there was a way to unify an approach, but it's impossible short of staying in structure and using the Buying Decision Funnel. The nature of buying decisions does not lend itself to one person making a quick decision in a vacuum, so the study of personality styles so prevalent in sales training today is not very helpful in Buying Facilitation.

As you bring your prospect down the Buying Decision Funnel, you will begin to note exactly how he needs to buy. First of all, he'll discuss how he's bought in the past. *A history of past buying patterns is a good indication of how people will buy in the future.* Compare what you've heard about the past patterns while prospects attempt to solve their current problem. You'll hear comments like the following:

"Traditionally, we've . . ."
"Our manager brought in this solution last year . . ."

"The human resources group takes care of that . . ."

"We have a team meeting every week . . ."

When you hear this information, ask more questions to see if they need to use those past patterns in solving their current problem.

"Do you need to follow that route this time?"

"Have you ever done it another way?"

"Are there any conditions under which others get involved?"

"Have you ever brought in another supplier to support you?"

Remember that the answers to these questions are not for you. They are for the prospect to decide how to move forward in his environment once he understands the problem and the Problem Space. *If you attempt to use your selling patterns at any point in the Buying Facilitation process, you will break rapport irreparably. People generally don't buy from people they don't like or trust.*

End your conversation with, "Where do you want to go from here?" Your prospect will tell you exactly how he wants to buy. You might not like the answer, but that's the deal. There is no other answer. Sellers who are used to making appointments won't like being told to be available for a conference call with the team. Sellers who like to make a pitch on their first call will feel out of control when asked to wait until the second call.

I personally do not like face-to-face visits as I can't get all the information I can get while sitting with my eyes closed, listening intently on the phone. *But if that is the way the prospect buys, it is my job to comply. That is what he needs to have happen to consider buying: it is his buying pattern.*

Remember: **You have nothing to sell if there's no one to buy. Relationship comes first. The buyer has the answers.** You are only the servant. If it will help, try to remember that there is no way you can know the complexity of the Problem Space, and that the prospect is addressing all of its components while seeking a solution. Respect that the prospect knows what he's doing, even if it doesn't fit in with your plans. Trust that he'll do what's right for himself, his company, his team. That's his job.

All you need to do is find someone who needs to buy. You have nothing to sell. Let your prospect tell you how, what, where, and when he wants to buy. Your job is to get out of Self, out of content, and out of your belief that it's your call. It's not.

SKILL SET #12:

Buying Patterns versus Selling Patterns

If you find that you follow a pattern over several calls—you open in a similar fashion, use similar sentences with similar results, expect a certain outcome from your communications—you are using a selling pattern.

Begin to notice any selling patterns you are currently using.

☐ Notice the different stages of your initial contact. Do you use an opening pitch? A script? What words do you use? Are they the same for every call? When do you vary your opening words? What are the results?

☐ Keep a journal of the ways your calls shift. At what point do you move from rapport building into the next phase? At what point in the call do you speak about your product? Is the prospect receiving your communication? How do you know? How does this vary? Why? When?

☐ Notice all the different phases of your prospecting calls. Recognize differences and similarities. Which ones work better than others? Why?

Start to be aware of buying patterns.

☐ Keep a record of how people buy. What are their patterns? Similarities? Differences? Who buys how, and when? What part did you play? How did you support this? Inhibit this?

☐ Who buys from you, in general? How do they do this? Why? How would they buy differently from someone else?

☐ Notice sales you thought you should have closed and didn't. Is there a pattern to these?

Start to get rid of your selling patterns and support people buying.

☐ Begin to use the Buying Decision Funnel through to its conclusion. What happens differently? What is the same? At what point do you get confused? Go into a pitch? Feel the need to have more control? Feel out of control?

☐ Watch yourself in the learning process. At what point do you want to go back to your selling patterns? Is there a pattern to your frustration? What would make you keep going through the learning curve?

☐ Notice how people need to buy. How do they show you the buying patterns they need to employ? How soon into the call are you aware of them? How do you support their patterns? Inhibit them?

☐ What do you need to do to enhance your ability to support a prospect's or team's buying patterns?

☐ What would have to happen for you to consider eliminating your selling patterns? What aspect(s) would you start with? What would be the most difficult to eliminate?

Chapter 10

Formulating the Right Questions

When I was in London, British Airways was one of my clients in my computer consultancy business. The vice president of user services and I were out to lunch one day. She mentioned that she had six data processing (DP) people who supported her users. Since I knew she had two thousand users, the user-to-programmer ratio seemed ridiculous to me. My initial inclination was to say,

"Hillary, how can that possibly work? How can six people provide all the services that two thousand people need? I think you need to bring in some of my people to help your DP people."

Given that the woman had responsibility for over two thousand people, I had to trust she was intelligent and had some clue how to solve her own problem. What I said instead was,

"How does that work?"

"I wish you hadn't asked me that," she said. "Now I'll have to address it. I've been kind of putting it out of my mind."

I smiled and changed the topic. I let go of my need to sell.

In the morning, I called her with an idea.

"I've been thinking. Can't British Airways supply you with one of their consultants so they can take a look around and see what's going on there?" *People buy only when they can't solve their own needs internally.*

"Thanks for thinking right along with me. I just placed a call to them to ask for one."

Two weeks later she called me to tell me she needed one of my analysts for at least three months. British Airways wouldn't be able to supply her with support for a year. It was a $150,000 job.

What did I do? Not a lot. I supported an intelligent person while she made her own decision. I asked her one question, which brought her brain to "search" mode and pushed her understanding that she had to find a solution to a problem. That's her job. It was always her solution: I was only the support person. *If I had assumed immediately that she needed my services, I might have put her on the defensive by not respecting her ability to solve her own problem.* Even if she acknowledged she needed the services my company provided, the disrespect I would have shown her would have impeded feelings of trust and rapport, and she might have looked into alternative suppliers.

I must admit that it was hard. It always is. I was trained as a stockbroker to use a traditional approach. My automatic response is to think that my product is the answer and that my selling prowess will win the day. But when I hear my internal dialogue giving me an answer to someone else's problem, making me believe that I know and she doesn't, I use that inner voice as a trigger to help me get into Observer and then formulate a question to get the prospect to look in the right direction for her own answer.

Our Questions Support the Buyer's Discovery

In the past, sellers have used questions to direct customers to look for the answer that the seller's product supplies. ("How would it be if there were a product that *could* do that?" or "Don't you think you should be looking at something more long term?") This type of question is seller-focused and product-based; it is used to provide the seller the information she needs to persuade or manipulate a prospect toward buying her product. In fact, when questions are used that way they put the prospect in a double bind: if the prospect answers truthfully, it might appear that she needs to purchase the product—which she may not have decided she needs to do yet—or look stupid. Or the prospect has to lie. This is how prospects get a reputation for being dishonest: they are actually defending themselves from being put in a no-win situation. In Buying Facilitation, our questions, formulated through the filter of providing service through discovery, can assist a prospect in achieving clarity in the problem–solution process.

In this chapter, you will learn the skills to formulate the questions that can lead the prospect to discover her solution—which may or may not be your product. Through your questions, you will be able to support the buyer in discovering the following:

- What the problem is.

- Where the problem resides within the Problem Space.

- How the problem was created and why.

- What keeps the problem going.

- What a Solution Space would look like.

- What needs to happen prior to a solution occurring.

- What is in place internally to solve the problem.

- Why the solution hasn't been tried before now.

- At what point it will be clear whether the internal solution will/will not solve the problem adequately.

- At what point an external solution will be sought.

- What criteria an external solution needs to meet.

- How an external solution would fit into the Problem Space.

- What an external solution would have to cover in order to be broad enough to encompass the Solution Space.

Unless it is an inexpensive or personal item that doesn't need a decision-making body for a decision, *it is not until all of these questions are addressed that a prospect can decide what is necessary to resolve her problem.*

It is possible—and highly likely—that through questioning, the prospect will discover how to solve her own problem with existing internal resources. *But she would have discovered that anyway—just farther along in the sales cycle, after several calls, proposals, hours spent by the seller trying to create a sale.* It's your job as a servant to help the prospect discover the easiest, most effective way to solve her own problem. This frees up both seller and prospect to move on.

Some prospects—the minority in my experience—are able to define their needs and proceed, effectively and efficiently, to purchase an external solution. These prospects will use your questions as a lever to catapult decision making. They are easy to work with: whether they decide to buy from you or not, the process is short.

With most prospects, however, you must deal not only with the issues that appear as problems in their environment, but also with the problems that have been created and exacerbated by intangibles, such as fear of change, company politics, or personal issues. Some examples might be long-term difficulties within the Problem Space that have become part of the company culture, such as a prospect who would rather maintain the status quo than admit her mistakes.

In either case, you must support the prospect's decision-making capability.

The Role of Beliefs and Values in Creating Change

Let's look at decisions and how they affect the problem and possible solution. Since all decisions encompass the beliefs and values of the decision-making body, each presented problem contains the beliefs and values that helped create it. For example, if someone purchased an inappropriate insurance policy, she did so for what seemed to be a good reason. Or if a team is not functioning effectively, it is a result of the beliefs and values that created the hiring practices and mandates used to form the team initially. Because the decisions that created the current, defined problem are not often recognized as part of the problem, prospects do not usually revisit their original decision-making process. Therefore, when prospects begin to look at their problematic environment, they limit their solution search to the content level and do not look at the full spectrum of what may need to be changed.

Sales people have generally not dealt with the beliefs and values that underlie the prospect's problems and decisions, and have focused on the content-specific problem their product can solve. They have actually missed the major decision-making markers.

In fact, when you focus on the prospect's stated problem, and do not go back and search at the beliefs and values level, you miss those same areas she is not attending to, in the same way that she is missing them, thereby aggravating the problem.

Prospects generally stay in content, looking at facts and details when initially describing their environment to someone they don't know or trust. But when your questions begin uncovering the underlying beliefs and values that have created the problem, prospects who are defending the company culture or protecting themselves will instead begin to ask *you* questions as an attempt to avoid answering. When they feel their beliefs are being challenged, they will resist change. But *change will occur only if beliefs are in place to support the change.*

Facilitative questions, the term I use for the overall category of questions in Buying Facilitation, examine beliefs and uncover underlying issues that helped exacerbate the problem. Until prospects can address those questions and their answers, and reexamine the underlying beliefs that helped them make the decisions that led them to their present state, they will not be in a position to consider buying, whether they need your solution or not.

Older Model Questions: What They Do

In most other sales techniques, questions have been a way to manipulate the buyer into some sort of discomfort, the alleviation of which comes with the purchase of the seller's product. I'd like to mention the most popular types and give you my beliefs about what happens in the buyer-seller interaction when they're used.

Open Questions

These questions have been taught as the most valuable questions to use: they are supposed to open up the conversation and dump all types of potentially usable information into the lap of the seller so she knows which route to take to close the deal. What these questions do, however, is create distrust. In the initial contact, when open questions are most often used, there is not enough rapport for the prospect to feel comfortable in answering truthfully. Furthermore, the seller loses control of the call while the buyer is discussing issues that may not be relevant to solving the problem. Most importantly, open questions also do not build the structure to lead the buyer to think sequentially about her problem.

Some examples of *open* questions:

> "How's it going?"
> "What happened?"
> "What are you planning on doing?"
> "What seems to be the problem? How are you going to fix it?"
> "What do you need to help you with that?"

The prospect can go in any direction she wishes with these and actually avoid those areas your product could serve. So if you sell kitchen equipment, she could talk about the chefs or the food suppliers. Basically, open questions aren't specific enough to bring the prospect from the problem to the Problem Space and through to the Solution Space.

Leading Questions

With leading questions, suggestions for action are contained within the question. Many sales strategies use questions that lead prospects to the answers the sellers want to elicit. These questions lead to distrust. More importantly, they don't get to the heart of the problem or help people buy—unless they are people who buy out of guilt and discomfort. Usually these questions are used on small ticket items, as they are short and hard hitting.

Some examples of *leading* questions:

> "You really should look at that, shouldn't you?"
> "Don't you think it's time to . . . ?"
> "Wouldn't you consider buying if I could prove that my product would help?"

Why Questions

These questions generally lead to defensiveness and rationalization of behavior. They also address the information already sitting in the white sock drawer—the information already on hand—and do not gather high-quality information.

Some examples of *why* questions:

> "I understand you are using widgets in your company. Why did you choose the brand you are using?"
> "I hear you are not getting your needs met with your current widgets. Why are you still using them?"

Facilitative Questions: What They Do

Facilitative questions are neither open questions (which encourage conversation but don't explore the full range of relevant information) nor closed questions (which provide clarity on a specific topic). When you ask Facilitative questions, you are setting up parameters that define and contain the territory to be explored and keep you within the area your product serves. Facilitative questions lead the prospect sequentially through her own maze of problems, solutions, answers, and resources, or potential decisions. They organize her brain, taking her from the white sock drawer to the colored sock drawer to the missing orange sock—to all the possibilities her problem creates.

Facilitative questions are based on values and outcomes, so they usually begin with "What" or "How." Again, the questions are created to direct the prospect toward her own answers. ***People buy only when they can't fill their own needs.***

Following are some generic examples of Facilitative questions to give you a general understanding of the type of information they elicit:

"What would you need to know to . . . ?"

"What would happen if . . . ?"

"What's important to you about . . . ?"

"What has stopped that from working before this?"

"What criteria would you use to choose?"

"What needs to happen differently—and what do you have in place to ensure that?"

"How would you know when it's the best time?"

"How would you do that?"

"How would you bring that into your environment? What would need to happen for it to work in the way you need it to work? How can you support that with the resources you have?"

"How would you know if . . . ?"

"How did you make that decision before?"

Notice how values, decision-making criteria, problems, and possible in-house solutions are examined in the above questions. Notice the assumption that the prospect can take care of all her own needs. *It is through this defined questioning that we can help the prospect quickly notice what's going on and get movement where necessary.*

Notice that these questions help the prospect move from the white sock drawer into the colored sock drawer. In order to move forward toward a solution, the prospect must find *specific answers*—which she often doesn't have prior to being asked the questions.

It is necessary to ask assumption-free questions, or the prospect will end up defending herself against an oncoming pitch rather than seeking answers. In this way, you can assist her in organizing and accessing all relevant, quality information, which is actually stored in her brain but is in the colored sock drawer.

Your job is to direct the questions to those areas in the colored sock drawer that (1) directly relate to your product and area of expertise; and (2) supply the appropriate high-quality information, and thereby define the parameters of the conversation by containing it within the area your product supports.

When I bought my new computer, one of the fun activities was to purchase new applications. I called a company to order one of their products and their order taker started telling me about all the specials they had. My $30 order was quickly looking like a $200 order. I coldly told her, "No, thank you. I'm fine." She then quietly asked me a killer question.

"Do you have any idea how you plan to keep your system clean and check out any problems that might be occurring that you don't know about?"

That was it, of course. She wasn't pushing a product any longer, but getting me to discover what I needed. Her question wasn't manipulative or self-serving, as in "I think you ought to consider using one of our other products to clean your system" or "Don't you think you ought to consider cleaning your system occasionally?" She didn't make me feel wrong or stupid, as I would have felt if she'd asked me "If you don't clean your system, do you know what could happen?" I felt she was supporting me in supporting myself. And I bought.

Formulating Facilitative Questions

As I said earlier, Facilitative questions are neither open nor closed questions but an interesting mixture of open, closed, general, and specific questions. They are a different type of question, certainly not the type we've been taught to ask. Learning how to create them and use them will take practice and patience.

To create them, you must stay curious and in Observer in order to explore the full range of possibilities. *As soon as you place parameters around any communication, as questions do by definition, you limit the possible answers to those that fit within your parameters.*

Here are some examples of specific Facilitative questions to give you an understanding of how to use them. Notice that the questions contain no content themselves, although they seek content-based information. In other words, Facilitative questions are formulated to provide the *structure* to assist the prospect in organizing her brain to find the specific information she needs to make a decision.

> "What are you doing in the way of sales training in your company right now?"
>
> "How does your team go about deciding how to work together on a network?"
>
> "Are there any conditions under which you would supplement your current insurance plans with additional ones?"
>
> "What is important to you about making a change at this time? What stopped you from considering it last year?"
>
> "How would you and your wife know when it was time to start doing your estate planning?"
>
> "How would your team decide to bring in a consultant?"
>
> "What process did your team go through to have that work out for everyone?"

Notice that none of these questions pushes product, although you can see clearly from the questions what the product is. None supplies answers, although they bring people to the place where they know where and how to look for answers. All of them trust that the prospect has the answer. As I say in *Sales on the Line*:

> The formulation of your questions should be structured to illuminate any problem areas that might exist in your client's environment. Your questions, therefore, should more clearly define your client's Present Situation and give you both a common understanding of the environment in which you might be working. (p. 90)

In fact, the questions can be asked in a way that helps the prospect sequentially order her thinking to get to the colored sock drawer quickly. These questions do not allow assumptions or subjective interpretations on the part of the seller. Historically, sellers have created their own scenarios to fit their needs, separate from the reality. They suffer the consequences through lost time and opportunities, then blame the prospect.

I recently heard a very funny story—funny, but sad.

A broker in a firm moved on, leaving behind several big accounts. One of her largest accounts was handed to a woman who was quite impressed with her own professional ability. She immediately called the client, who was halfway across the country.

> "Hello. This is ABC company. May I help you?"
>
> "Oh, hello. My name is Jane Jones, and I've taken over for Sandra Smith at Hutchinson & Co. Is Mr. Roberts in?"
>
> "No, I'm sorry, he's not."
>
> "Well, I called to tell him that I'll be in your area next Thursday and I thought I'd drop in and introduce myself in person. Would you be open to that?"
>
> "Sure. I'd be glad to meet you. I'll be here all day Thursday, so come on by."
>
> The broker got on a plane, stayed in a hotel, rented a car, and found her way to the client. When she got there, she was gaily greeted by the receptionist. After ten minutes of chat, she asked to see the client.
>
> "Oh, he's on vacation for the next two weeks. I thought since you were here in town anyway, we could spend a few minutes together, considering I take some of his calls."
>
> The broker forgot to ask if the man would be in town.

It's amazing how we hear what we want to hear. If we are able to open up the parameters and explore relevant information, we just might be able to assemble all the elements in the Problem Space on the first call.

A note of caution: in the past, asking questions may have given you control over the type of answers you got. This was both good and bad because you probably created *and* hampered sales with your questions. In fact, through your questions you may have created scenarios to fit your own needs, and then lost time and opportunities when those scenarios were inaccurate. Sellers often blame the prospect when their questions don't evoke what they consider to be the appropriate response.

With Facilitative questions, you have control; it is just a different type of control. In fact, you end up with more control because you affect the direction and structure of the conversation. You never had control of the outcome of the call anyway. You just liked to think you did.

How Facilitative Questions Move Buyers to Discover Answers

In my computer consulting company, I continually heard the technical people talk about how stupid the users were. "They asked for this. When I gave it to them, after spending six months writing the program, they told me it wasn't what they wanted." I began to think there was something wrong other than the user being "stupid." As a test, I called in my head technician and asked her to design a program for me. She was ready; we'd talked about it for a year.

> "Great. So what do you want?"
> "I don't know."
> "Well, from what I've heard you say, you're looking for . . ."

I listened while she went ahead and put forth a plan which, if executed, would have given me the wrong system. She never again asked me questions of any relevance and worked from the assumption that she had the answers. I finally stopped her.

"How would you have approached our interaction if you believed I knew the answer to your first question?"

"But you didn't. You said you didn't know."

"I didn't know how to answer your question, but I can hear that what you're saying is wrong. I just don't know how to have my brain get it all out to you."

We worked on a set of questions that would help me—and other clients—access information in a way that would provide me the information I needed to know to help me get my problem solved. Ultimately, the conversation went like this:

"I hear you are looking for a system to track sales. Do you have any idea of what it will do for you when we are done creating it?"

"I want it to let me know when to call clients back, when they are due for their 'hello' calls, and where they are in the sales cycle."

"Do you have any idea of how you'd like to have that information available to you?"

"I'd love it if I could write in a name and have several options of what information I needed, then push a button and call up the right screen."

"Do you have a picture in your mind of what that screen would look like?"

In this way, my technical manager led me through all the pos-sibilities and issues she would have to deal with in order to cre-ate what I wanted. She knew where to direct me to look since she knew what was possible. She had the questions, and I had the answers. When my answers wouldn't work for her, she used the information they contained to find a more appropriate one.

Once she moved from believing she had the answers herself to trusting that I had the answers, her questions had to be directed toward discovering the possible answers, and formulated in a way that pointed my brain in the direction to search. ***The buyer has the answers, the seller has the questions.***

How to Choose What to Say

When I start my questioning process with prospects or clients, I start with their current environment. Where are they now? Once we both get a good look at where they are and how they got there, I follow the direction of the Buying Decision Funnel.

But I do more than just ask questions. In fact, people need to stand back and take the Observer position in order to get perspective. I use the questioning process to assist them in doing that. But there are actually three things I can do when it's my turn to speak—remembering that conversations go in turns. I can either *ask a question, agree,* or *summarize.* Since we've been spending time on asking questions, let's look at *agreeing* and *summarizing.*

When prospects make statements such as, "We have the best way of doing that!" or "We've been doing it that way for the past three years and it really seems to be working," I agree by saying, "That sounds wonderful" or "I'm so glad for you" or "That's impressive." Make no mistake, *I absolutely mean what I am saying.* If you were speaking with a friend and she told you the same thing, would you doubt her? Would you challenge her as some sales approaches recommend? Why would you think of doing that with someone who might not use your product because she is happy with what she's already doing? Good for her! How many of us are clear that what we are doing is the right thing?

It is okay for people not to need our product. We can't sell to everyone we speak with. Our job is to find those who do need our product, not create a buyer from an unqualified prospect.

Sometimes, my agreement gives a prospect who seems to be doing just fine the ability to step back and take a further look: "But you know, as I think about that I'm realizing . . ." Then more information comes out and I can bring the prospect further down the Funnel by basing my next questions on the new information. I never know which way it will go, but I respect and trust the process.

The other choice I have, besides asking a question or agreeing, is to summarize.

After a few questions, just to make sure I have understood the information so I can proceed to formulate questions using accurate information, I repeat what I believe I have heard. Often it's accurate, sometimes not. But this gives prospects another way to move back and be an Observer. It's very powerful. Just about every time I summarize, prospects add information they forgot the first time. "Right! Exactly. And what happens *then* is . . ."

I use the information people share only as a basis from which to ask future questions, to know where to direct the information gathering. Compare this with the older selling strategies, which use information as a way to close a sale or to persuade. Prospects become afraid of answering the older types of questions, knowing the information will be used against them, but have no apprehension in answering Facilitative questions as these so obviously serve their own process of discovery.

It doesn't take long before prospects trust that the way I am selling to them is supportive rather than manipulative. I often hear prospects say things like, "Boy, this is great. You ask great questions." Or "I haven't thought of this before. Thanks." One prospect called back moments after I ended a call and said, "Were you just *doing it* to me? Is that what you are selling? The way you just *did* that? If you can teach my people how to do that, you're hired. I'm still thinking about some of the questions you asked."

People are good. They would much prefer to trust and collaborate. It's pretty amazing how quickly they offer their willingness to engage in the Buying Decision Funnel and become part of a "We Space" with me.

The most difficult part of the questioning process is knowing the right questions to ask. While it seems paradoxical, your prospect will actually let you know where to go next and whether to question, agree, or summarize. All you have to do is listen for the clues in what she is really saying and stay out of content.

I recently spoke with a client who had been using parts of Buying Facilitation mixed with other Consultative sales approaches. She admitted that she uses Facilitative questions as a way of making her usual Consultative selling approach more effective, but was having difficulty closing. "They can't make decisions. They don't know how to buy," she told me.

I asked her a few questions:

- ■ "Are you working with their values, their culture, their beliefs?"

- ■ "How did their Problem Space get created?"

- ■ "Under what conditions will it change?"

- ■ "What needs to happen for something to be different?"

- ■ "How would they use your product?"

- ■ "How would they bring it in-house? Why should they? Whose toes would it step on? Who would lose their job?"

- ■ "What would happen to the management team with your product in place? The employees?"

- ■ "How will they make a decision?"

"Why don't you know the answers to these questions?"
She answered: "I guess that's why I'm not closing any sales."

SKILL SET #13:

Using Questions to Support Discovery

During your selling sessions, begin to notice how you are currently asking questions.

☐ Notice what your intent behind each question is. Is it to convince? Support? Manipulate? Gather information so you can use it in your pitch?

Write down as many of the questions you use as you can think of. Begin to track which ones you use most often. Notice what types of responses you are getting to the questions you are asking.

☐ Log the gist of the responses. If you find it difficult, get into Observer by standing up while on the phone. Begin to see patterns in responses: when you ask *this* type of a question you get *that* response.

Ready yourself for changing the outcome of your calls and the intent of your questions.

☐ Begin by clearing your brain of any proscribed outcome for the calls. Understand that your job is to serve your prospect in discovering how best to solve any problems using her own resources.

Begin using the Buying Decision Funnel.

☐ Start noticing differences between using the Funnel and asking your more traditional questions. Notice where you get stuck and why.

☐ Notice which of your old questions reappear when you feel stuck. Notice the differences in the responses and level of trust you are creating.

Learn to move between agreement, questioning, and summarizing.

☐ Let the conversation flow naturally. Your prospect's responses will tell you which questions to use. Trust your instincts.

☐ Notice when your need to direct the call to the content of your product comes in. Notice the differences in the conversation.

Chapter 11

Listening Skills

We have worked with questions as a way to engender a trusting collaboration and now we will learn about the role of listening in that same process. Listening includes some of the skills from chapter 9, skills we used to define the boundaries of our job as servants, including structure and content, Self and Observer. In this chapter, we'll learn specifically how to perform these skills.

The Listening Systems

In order to get the information you need to serve, support discovery, and continue an ongoing win-win collaboration with prospects, you need to be able to *listen*, to hear and understand both what was said and what was meant. In order to assist you in learning the listening process, I have divided it into three main components.

Listening is a system of chosen auditory behaviors that involve knowing how to

- select the precise parts of a message to listen to and navigate between the words and their intent (*system of navigation*);

- understand the meaning behind the message (*system of awareness*);
- deliver a response that lets a person know he has been heard (*system of delivery*).

Let's look at how these systems work together.

System of Navigation

Moving between Different Perspectives:
Self, Observer, Neutral

The first component in listening is the system of navigation, which means taking the *responsibility to move around among the different perspectives* in order to

- skillfully gather the necessary information,
- accurately make sense of it, and
- deliver our response appropriately.

In other words, hear what's being said, understand it accurately, and respond in kind. In order to have conscious choice in your communication, you must be able to choose to be an *Observer,* which allows you to gain the necessary objectivity. But if you enter into a dialogue with your prospect from the Observer mind set, you'll be hovering over your conversation rather than actively engaged in it. As I discussed in chapter 9, you must be able to *decide* from *Observer*—make your mental calculations and formulate your responses—but *deliver* the words from *Self,* in order to *be* with your prospect in a personal way.

In addition, there are times during a conversation when you need to just let information in, without deciding anything, thinking anything, or delivering anything. I call that place *Neutral.* This third perspective of the listening system of navigation deals with nonverbal messages.

Neutral and Nonverbal Cues

During the first part of a phone call or visit, when the prospect is beginning to talk about what is generally going on in the area your product serves, you have no real information with which to know how to move forward or formulate questions. While much of this book deals with ways to gather essential *verbal* information, you also need the available *nonverbal* information.

Gathering nonverbal information is much like sitting in front of a TV while fixing a tennis racket or listening to a CD play music in the background while you're working: you know the information is there, but not at a level of specificity that gets you deeply involved with the content.

When asking the initial round of questions on the top half of the triangle (see illustration on page 124), you don't need to know the content anyway—the prospect does. You just need enough information to formulate the next question to help him decide where he needs to go next in his brain.

In Neutral, you can listen or watch for any available nonverbal information that might help you to take responsibility for the interaction. There is a vast array of nonverbal messages that will give you clues on how to proceed: comfort level, willingness to engage, agreement, disagreement, understanding and misunderstanding, annoyance, acceptance, distrust. To understand these messages, you must feel them from your intuition or from watching, listening, and reading between the lines.

Is the person stressed? Busy? Easy-going? Friendly? Difficult? Cautious? You need this information to stay in rapport, to make next-step decisions:

- What is the real meaning of what is being said?
- Is this a person I want to work with?
- What are the underlying values here? Are they similar enough to mine to want to work together?

Traditionally, Westerners have not been trained to value information that comes from our guts: the left-brain, scientific model is the primary paradigm our culture gives merit to. Yet we each emanate vast amounts of valuable information that is crucial to hearing and understanding each other. As a seller, your job demands that you have the information you need to assist your prospects. You therefore have to add the nonverbal elements to the equation. Without them, you don't have the complete picture.

Remember that people are all always communicating something, whether they speak or not. Think of your dog, your cat, your horse, your bird. Don't you know what he needs? Just because he's not using words doesn't mean he's not communicating. So it is with people. As a seller you need to use and fine-tune your ability to read people and situations.

I offer some caution, however. It is easy to misread or misinterpret nonverbal cues, especially when you are new at it. Check it out. Use your summary questions to make certain you have made an accurate assessment of what you think is going on.

System of Awareness

Forms of Information:
Structure, Content, Meta-Message

The system of awareness *makes it possible for the seller to assist the prospect in doing a mental search* for the appropriate information. Through the components of awareness—structure, content, and meta-message—the missing bits, the "Ahas!" will be discovered.

The *structure* of a conversation is the container, while the *content* gives the details (the ice cream and the ice cream cone, as we discussed in chapter 9). The seller stays in structure while supporting the prospect's discovery, and only moves to content once the prospect discovers whether the seller's product would potentially provide a solution. The *meta-message* is the unspoken meaning.

In *Sales on the Line* I say:

> Listening for content gives me the issues the person is willing to let me know about. Listening for the meta-message gives me the underlying problems the person faces. (p. 117)

When listening, it is easy for sellers to confuse the content with the meta-message: to confuse what is being *said* with what is *meant*.

Meta-messages

Generally there is meaning behind the spoken word that conveys a person's entire value system. The problem is that when people receive messages through words, they interpret the words according to their own internal value system. If the internal systems are disparate, and most of us are very different, then understanding is blurred by the listener's own beliefs in regard to that same word usage. In other words, people don't understand each other a lot.

When I lived in London I was invited to go on a walk. The group called me several times to make sure I had the right equipment. I bought what they suggested: a rucksack (backpack), a cagoul (windbreaker), and sturdy boots. I was mystified why I needed all that equipment to go for a walk. When I questioned it, I was told the weather was so changeable I needed to be prepared. Sure enough, when we got to the spot, the wind came up, the clouds opened, and rain descended. I could barely see a foot in front of me. Thank heaven I had my equipment! As we began our walk I noticed we were going on an upward slope, which soon became a steep incline. I was hanging on to whatever rock I could find to maintain my footing.

"This isn't a 'walk.' We're mountain climbing!" I shouted.

"Of course. Walk, mountain climb—same thing."

I would never have gone mountain climbing if I had known.

Let's look at a few of the more obvious meta-messages in sales:

"I'm kind of busy, but I've got a few minutes, what's up?" means, *"I'll speak to you if it's worth my time."*

"Send me some material," means, *"I'm trying to get you off the phone so you'll stop bothering me and this is the only way I know how to do it."*

"Call me next week, after I've received the material and had a chance to look it over. Then I'll have a better idea of where we're at," means, *"When I get the material, I'll review it with the team and then we'll decide if we really need to go external to fix the problem and if we do, then I'll look at your product and all the others I can find."*

It is imperative that you understand the *intent* of what the buyer is saying, rather than *your interpretation* of the words.

Understanding Accurately

In order to understand that my version of what has been said is accurate, there are two things I do: (1) I go into Observer (which gives me the ability to gain perspective without personal involvement), and/or (2) I present a summary statement (to get my understanding affirmed).

> "Did I just hear you say . . ."
> "So what you are saying is . . ."
> "It sounds to me like what's happening is . . ."

I do *not* necessarily repeat the exact words I've heard the prospect say; I summarize what I believe the previous few moments of the conversation were about, using both content and meta-message. The summary actually moves the conversation down the Buying Decision Funnel by putting the prospect in Observer and allowing him to see his environment through my eyes. His answer to my summary gives me an accurate understanding of what I think I've heard, so I can formulate my next question. Because people have a fairly accurate picture of the pieces of their current environment and what the specific problem looks like, summarizing every few interactions moves them beyond the obvious, helps them to find new ways to look at existing information, and brings out their unformulated plans, which are based on guesswork and assumptions. By summarizing, I help him get the potential reality on the table: what's missing, what's in the way of a solution, what's possible or not.

A client of mine was complaining about one of his regular senior management meetings. Senior managers were not getting information to him regularly, the meetings were frequently rescheduled, people were late. The meta-message I was hearing was that there was something going on internally between him and the team that was creating friction and avoidance.

We took a good look at the current history of the management team, and discovered issues around my client's recent reorganization of his staff—a reorganization that created much dissension and national controversy. When I asked him to look at some of those issues in relation to the team, he replied, "Oh, that has nothing to do with them. Besides, I made the decisions on my own so they wouldn't have to take any of the flack."

By leading him through the Buying Decision Funnel, he was able to discover that his solution had not been big enough for the Problem Space and he had left behind several unresolved issues as a result.

I was able to use the information from the meta-messages I heard to direct him where to look to solve his problem. I wouldn't have had enough information on the content level to have helped him adequately. By communicating with him in the form of content-free statements—the structure—I was able to stay out of his personal issues and support his understanding.

On all levels of listening with awareness—structure, content, and meta-message—it is necessary to move between the three to get a complete picture of the situation, which leads me to the final system of listening.

System of Delivery

Multiple Modes of Communication:
Sender and *Receiver*

The System of delivery ensures that you respond to your prospect in a way that lets him know you have heard him. One of the fundamental laws of communication is that if there is no receiver, there is no communication. If it weren't for my understanding that sales has worked from a task base, I would be mystified as to why sales training has taught opening pitches for so long—because when a seller opens with a pitch, *there is no receiver.*

I often ask my training course participants, "Do you want to speak or do you want to have someone hear you? Which?"

When you are presenting a product or pitching, you are a **sender** with no **receiver.** No one listens because *they don't know how to listen or what to listen for.* Pitches were created as part of the task-based, product-focused, and seller-based sales strategies. Using a pitch in the upper Funnel perpetuates the numbers game aspect of sales since the seller is merely lucky if the prospect wants to take the time to listen.

In order for your prospects to trust, to feel in relationship, to feel heard, they must have some way of comprehending that you are supporting them, which means you must communicate your support in ways by which they understand they are being served. After all, *just because you believe you are sending a message doesn't mean it is being received.*

Until now, sales methodologies have put the seller and his sales patterns directly in the way of the prospect's discovery. But in a communication, there is a sender and a receiver, or it's not considered a communication.

Assuring There Is a *Receiver*

Every strategy, tactic, and approach taught in sales training, until now, has taught only one side of the communication equation, without taking in the full collaboration. To know there is a receiver when you are communicating, you must watch for the following communication clues:

Phone Sales

Shifts in voice—tone, rhythm, volume, tempo

Shifts in language patterns—types of words, length of sentences

Changes in breathing—loud sighs or no discernible breathing

Face-to-Face Sales

Shifts in body language—posture, arms, sitting back or forward, breathing

Shifts in gestures—large to small, small to large, stopping, starting

Shifts in facial features—skin changes, jaw movements, mouth, eyes

Shifts in voice—tone, rhythm, volume, tempo

Shifts in language patterns—types of words, length of sentences

Changes in breathing—watch for movement in chest area

When you notice something is shifting, changing from what it was moments before, you know that something different has just happened. It should be apparent whether the change was positive or negative. You must be aware of the shifts and take responsibility for your role in creating a shift. Many of us have a long history of blaming the other person for not understanding us, rather than taking responsibility for being understood.

I went to visit a new friend recently and got hopelessly lost with the directions he gave me. When I got there I said, "I had a hard time following your directions. The words you used were difficult for me to understand."

"I gave the directions just fine. You just couldn't follow them."

When I repeated what I had originally said—that I couldn't make sense of his words—not that he had made a mistake in the way they were offered, he got quiet. Then he said, "So what would you have needed to hear from me to have had them make more sense?"

Assuring You Are Heard

As a seller, you must take the responsibility to make sure you speak in a way you are heard. You must continually check on the "We Space" to make sure the prospect is in there with you. Because prospects usually don't know how to uphold their end of the "We Space" (nor do they know you well enough initially to want to), it is your job to make sure that the ideas communicated from both ends of the conversation are understood. In the above example, my new friend—as the "seller" of directions—didn't take the responsibility to make sure he was heard. As the "buyer," I didn't know any better and didn't know that I didn't know until it was too late. If my friend had taken the responsibility to make sure he had been heard, he would have asked me to repeat the directions as I understood them, and he would have recognized the error.

Until now, sellers have not been given the responsibility to make sure they are heard in a way that supports discovery and maintains rapport.

This point is an important one. Most of us growing up in the last two generations were taught that people felt or reacted however they did because it was their "stuff," as we said in the sixties, and it had nothing to do with us. Let me offer a metaphor I use to teach this concept.

Let's say I am speaking with someone and use the simple word "blue." As soon as he hears the word, my communication partner gets upset. The two traditional reactions I would have would be to say either:

"What's your problem? All I said was 'blue.' There's no reason to get upset with a word that's just a color." Or,

"You're getting upset over that? That's ridiculous. You want to be upset? Be my guest. Just don't blame me."

Sound familiar?

In fact, there's another way to address this issue. Because I believe in a "We Space" that sender and receiver share, I believe we share responsibility for each other. Because the receiver, in this case the prospect, doesn't have enough history with you to have the desire to take responsibility around his share of the communication, you must take that responsibility initially. Eventually, as the prospect becomes a buyer and client, he will share this responsibility.

Given that part of your job as seller is to take responsibility for the interaction in general, you must create the environment in which a prospect can discover how best to get his needs met. If he becomes annoyed by something you say (even if it appears rational to you), *you must take the responsibility to go into the middle of the problem and alleviate it.* If you don't, you have broken rapport irreparably. It's not about right; it's about relationship.

In the above instance, I'd say something like, "I see that when I used the word 'blue' I caused a reaction. Want to tell me about it?" I am taking responsibility for a more complete, and potentially healing, dialogue without taking responsibility for the prospect's feelings. The prospect might tell me that when he was three years old his dog Blue died in his arms, and that might have caused the reaction. It might be that the ex-shop-foreman named John Blue is causing a major lawsuit. *You don't know what the cause of the reaction is, and you're not responsible for creating the feelings, but the fact that you said the word(s) that created the problem means you must do something to create the solution or you may lose the prospect as a result of the loss of rapport.*

Assuring a "We Space"

How many times have you been having a good call or meeting with a prospect and then something happens that creates discomfort but isn't addressed? You go to call the prospect back and he doesn't return your call. He's a jerk, right? Wrong. You could have fixed it.

Briefly stated: *when there's a problem, go in and fix it. If you don't, the damage may be irreparable.*

When you and your prospect have an uncomfortable issue between you that has come up in the conversation and you don't deal with it, the fact that it hasn't been dealt with doesn't mean it goes away. It just sits there between you, and there is a serious break in rapport. In this case, the prospect is the sender and you must be the receiver and deal with it. Remember that you are working toward creating a "We Space."

When you take the responsibility to go back in and mention that you've noticed a problem, there's a chance to dissolve the problem and go forward. If nothing is said, there will most likely be an end to the relationship. If you bring it up, there will most likely be an end to the problem. We have never before been taught, as sellers, to take this level of responsibility; instead, we blame the problem on the prospect and don't make a sale as a result. Neither seller nor prospect wins in that situation.

When you put these three listening systems together—navigation, awareness, and delivery—you can truly hear your prospect and he can feel heard. These skills give you a major piece of the responsibility you must take to create a collaboration. You will be putting these skills together, along with the rest of the skills that create collaboration, in chapter 12.

SKILL SET #14:

Listening to Support a Trusting Collaboration

Begin to notice how you listen and record what you notice in your journal. Practice all three listening systems in your personal life during the course of a week.

☐ What are you listening for when you are in conversation with your family and friends? Are you listening for an opening in order to speak? Are you listening for content?

☐ Begin to notice the structure of conversations when people speak to you from content. How difficult is it for you to remove yourself from the content to hear the structure? If you have difficulty, place yourself in Observer. Notice the difference. When can you easily be in structure? When is it difficult? What's the difference?

☐ Move back and forth between Self, Observer, and Neutral in your conversations with family and friends for a week. Keep a record each day. Note successes and failures. Specifically notice what you did when it worked and what you did when it didn't work. What's easy? What's hard? Are there types of conversations that are easier to navigate than others? Be specific. It's important to know the skills you use in order to replicate them while on sales calls.

☐ When you are sending a message, notice if your message is being received. Notice how you know when a family member or friend is in a "We Space" with you. Record the specific communication clues you notice when you know that someone is listening to you and that you are being heard. How do those clues differ from when someone recognizes that you are hearing them?

Begin to bring these skills to your work environment.

☐ Start by noticing how you send and receive messages with current clients. With prospects? How does this differ from the way you communicate with family or friends?

☐ Begin noticing how you send and receive messages with prospects. What are the differences?

Begin to use your new skills.

☐ Notice which skills feel most comfortable to begin trying. Which feel least comfortable? Make a list of all of the skills in this chapter in the order of comfort, with the most comfortable first. Notice the resistance to learning the uncomfortable ones. Practice each skill until it is comfortable.

☐ What happens to your conversations when you use these skills? Note as many specifics as possible. Note the skills you used in each instance to support enhanced collaboration.

☐ Practice the listening systems. Notice the difference in the amount of information you take in now versus prior to using the systems. How specifically does this change your interactions?

What skills are you still missing that will help you support your prospects or clients better?

☐ Notice areas of confusion that don't abate within two days. Record these areas. Practice other skill sets within this book to alleviate the confusion and build your skills for a week, then go back to your areas of confusion and try again.

III

Being a Buying Facilitator

In this final section, the beliefs and skills of Buying Facilitation will be combined into the application, addressing such questions as:

- How, when, why, and where do you do it?
- How do you use all the pieces we've learned throughout the book?
- What does it look like when you bring it to work?

Included are complete scenarios, as well as the thinking process I go through when using Buying Facilitation.

Chapter 12

Using Buying Facilitation:
Putting the Skills Together

Now you know the beliefs of Buying Facilitation and how it is different from the older approaches, as well as the skills of Buying Facilitation supporting discovery, listening, and asking questions. In this chapter, I'd like to introduce the application of Buying Facilitation by leading you through the process step-by-step and offering you my thinking as I go through a sales call.

The Step-by-Step Process

To support your learning, I have broken the following dialogue into numbered segments, with an explanation of what I am doing in each segment. I am using the telephone as the medium for a cold call as most sales at least begin on the phone. A cold call can be used to gather enough appropriate information to save a seller much time going out on inappropriate visits.

To make it easier to follow the interaction, I will begin with the prospect answering the call herself—a rare event. I will put forth a simple example of how this all works so you can get a picture of the complete process. The prospect answers the phone:

"Hi there."

1."Hi there. **2.** This is Sharon Drew Morgen. Who am I speaking with please?"

"This is Martha Smith."

3. "Hello. I'm with ABC Corporation and this is a sales call. **4.** Is this a good time to speak?"

---

1. Here I am starting the conversation by matching voice and greeting as a way to begin setting up rapport. People notice differences, not similarities, so I enter at the comfort level of my prospect. The only way to do this on the phone is through voice. If you are in person, match body posture.

2. Even if I have the name of the person in front of me, I don't assume I know how to address this person. People have preferences as to how they want to be addressed. They have nicknames and funny pronunciations. Nothing will get you out of rapport with a stranger faster than either mispronouncing or calling her a wrong name.

3. I *always* tell my prospect that this is a sales call. She will know it anyway. I'm not her sister, mother, friend, or colleague. Also, it's not a service call or an opportunity call. Those words are all fudging the truth to make it more palatable, given that sales people have such a bad reputation at this point in time. The truth is, it is a sales call. And I am a servant. Honesty goes a long way toward setting up a trusting environment.

4. People are busy. They are not sitting around waiting for you to call unless it has been prearranged. *If you don't ask if they are busy, you are disrespecting their time.* I know you've been taught to get in with a mesmerizing opening. If your prospect is doing something else, she won't hear you anyway. You become a sender with no receiver. The fact that you have matched her voice, asked her name, and asked about her time availability gives your prospect the meta-message that you respect her and are not attempting to get your needs met at her expense. When you use all of the above skills to open the call, the prospect will feel safe enough to speak honestly with you, or give you a more convenient time to call back, without feeling she is going to be abused by your agenda.

5. MS:"I've got a few minutes. What are you selling?"

6. SDM: "Training. But I don't know if you need to buy anything so I'd like to ask you a few questions. **7.** If we decide to speak for more than a few minutes and it cuts into your time, just let me know and we can end the call when it's convenient for you."

8. MS:"Thank you. I'll let you know. What are you selling?"

---

5. Prospects are afraid to commit too much time since they know it's a sales call. Please note: *If she had said she was busy, I would have quickly said, "What's a good time to call back?"* Because I have shown her that I respect her time, she would have been glad to give me another time to call back. *I have never had a busy prospect on a cold call try to ditch me once she was aware of my level of respect.*

6. I don't pitch; I just simply answer the question. She is not a receiver at this point, so a description of what I sell would fall on deaf ears. I also want her to know that I clearly understand that if she has nothing to buy I have nothing to sell. I am not trying to manipulate a sale, I am trying to locate an appropriate buyer who would be well served to buy my product.

7. Notice my use of the word "we." Notice that I offer her permission to not speak with me if it will disrupt her in any way. *Notice how this sets up a "We Space."* The meta-message is not only that I am respecting her time, but that I am not trying to abuse the privilege she's offered by being willing to speak with me. My job is to serve her; I want her to know that.

8. She has agreed to join a "We Space" with me, as evidenced by her willingness to participate. For those of you using opening statements, you will be used to more hostile receptions. In fact, this really is the response you get when using Buying Facilitation.

9. SDM: "My company sells sales training. Could you please tell me what you are doing in the way of sales training in your company?"

MS:"Well, we've got an in-house program that we run a few times a year for the new hires. It's brought in by the national team."

10. SDM: "Is it meeting your needs?"

MS: "Pretty much. It's what they give us, and we don't have to pay for it. It's okay. We meet our quotas."

11. SDM: "So I hear you saying that you have a free national program that you use regularly, that it helps you meet your quotas, and that you're not particularly crazy about it."

MS: "Right. I can't complain, though, our sales are doing well."

12. SDM: "Have you ever brought in outside sales training?"

---

9. and **10.** Here I am getting Martha to take a good look at her Present Situation. I am also starting to help her find the elements in the Problem Space that seems to be presenting itself. If she had said, "We've got this amazing training, and we are 50 percent over the national average. We just love it!" there would not be a presenting Problem Space to examine. At that point I would have asked one final question before ending the call: "Are there any conditions under which you would consider using additional sales training to supplement what you are currently doing?" But her meta-message is that there's something missing that she may not be able to do anything about because it's tied in with her national corporation.

11. This is a summary statement.

12. I am continuing to look at the Present Situation. If she's not completely satisfied *and* she has no choice to do anything different, there is no way to continue. If she has a choice and hasn't used that option, that's an important piece of information for both of us.

MS: "We have. I don't know if it's been any more successful than what we've got, but we brought in a program just last year."

13. SDM: "How did you decide to bring in another program?"

---

13. This is a vital question. It will give us both her potential buying patterns. *Notice I am in structure and Martha is in content. Note the power of staying in structure: I am in control of the direction of the call, and using that control to have her sequentially order her thinking in the area of my product expertise.*

14. MS: "I think it's important to keep abreast of what's going on. What type of sales training do you do? Is it new?"

---

14. This is an important response. It tells us both her criterion for choice (keeping up with new trends), as well as one of the elements for determining how to buy. Notice she has come back at me with a question. This often happens when a prospect begins to get uncomfortable because an area appears that shows less success than she'd like. It is an interesting point in the conversation, since it's not time for me to answer (she doesn't know what she needs yet, or if she is willing to explore training with me), but she needs to know we are in rapport for us to move forward. Although she sounds curious, she doesn't have enough understanding of what she needs to be able to determine if what I do fits into her idea of "new" or "training."

15. SDM: "Our training is revolutionary, I think, and I can't wait to tell you about it, but I don't really know yet if you even need anything. Could you tell me under what conditions you might consider bringing in additional training? It's sounding to me like you are doing fine with what you have."

---

15. We've determined Martha's Present Situation (in-house, corporate, and mediocre training) and that she's potentially missing something (could do better, likes new material) and hasn't been happy with what she's tried. If she decides to bring in more training, she will need to make decisions with her people. *Notice I did not go into a pitch, although she's asked for one. This is a trap. She is not a receiver yet, doesn't know what or if she needs to buy, and is still very much in the discovery phase.* If I answer her request for a pitch at this time, I will be moving out of rapport and pitching what I want her to buy rather than what she might need. *Again, she has no recognized needs at this point so I have nothing to sell.*

By answering my question about the conditions under which she might bring in additional training, Martha moves us to the Future side of the Buying Decision Funnel. We will now begin to get acquainted with the Problem Space and the culture it identifies. I gave her agreement so she would take a moment to look again at what she's got in place to make sure she'd be willing to go through the hassle required to do something different. Notice we are at the point in the Buying Decision Funnel at which the team is introduced.

16. MS: "We are doing okay but I like us to stay fresh, to keep learning. Our home office doesn't bring in new blood very often, so I stay on the lookout for new skills to add to what we are doing. To bring in new training, I'd need approval from home office, but

I have my own budget. Frankly, I'd need to know that what you've got would make a difference. You'd have to convince me as well as my sales manager that we would benefit from your training."

---

16. Note how far down the Funnel Martha has come. She has determined she can't fix what she's got using internal resources, and why, when, and what she'd consider for an external solution. Now she must determine how she'll choose an external solution and how to bring it into her group.

17. SDM: "I'd need to know a bit more specifically what you have in the way of training right now in order to know if what we're doing is any different. Our training is very unique and doesn't suit every environment. Could you tell me what type of training you are doing now? What approaches you are using? What specific areas you think could benefit from additional help?

---

17. Notice that I still am not presenting my product since neither of us know what she needs addressed. I don't want to ignore her, so I am commenting briefly on her questions. Notice also that I have gone *back up the Funnel* to have us take a closer look at the Present and Desired Situations. I'd like to point out yet again that I am still in structure, that I have left the content to Martha, and that I am strictly enforcing control on the call. Martha and I are staying tightly within the Funnel. In fact, this conversation has gone on less than five minutes. Notice the level of trust and collaboration. Martha has to be feeling the respect I am giving her for her ability to solve her own problems. I have not taken the opportunity—presented three times, including her opening question—to pitch my product, since my job is not product-focused. Each time I go back in to support her discovery, our rapport and "We Space" grows.

MS: "We are doing a combination of several Consultative approaches. Since we believe that face-to-face visits are necessary, we could use some help qualifying prospects better to have a higher closing ratio. Could you do that?"

18. SDM: "Actually, that's exactly what we do: help prospects decide how they want to buy, just as I'm doing with you. Could you tell me what else you'll need to know about our work so I could give you the complete information? Is there something I need to know about your team to address any decisions you'd have to make about bringing me in?"

---

18. Again, we still don't have enough information for me to present. I still need to know how she's going to buy if it's appropriate.

19. MS: "I'd need to have a meeting with you and the team so they can ask you questions and be satisfied that we're not just bringing in someone who will waste their time. We'd need some way of knowing that you could help with the qualifying process. Could you give me names of companies in our field who have used you? If we decide to go forward, we'd need to know how you follow up so we won't be left with all these new ideas and no one to help clear up the confusion."

20. SDM: "I hear that you would like to know what type of training we do, how we would work with your team, what types of referrals I could give you, what type of follow-up we'd provide, and that it is important for you to get training that will help you be more successful than you already are. I'd love to tell you what we're doing. Do you still have time?"

---

19. and **20.** Now she's ready. We've come down the Funnel. She knows exactly what she needs, how she needs it, what criteria she'd use to make a decision, how to bring the solution into the environment, how to know if we'd be the ones she'd choose. At this point, I would present my product, making sure to address all the points in my summary.

The Funnel widens out here. After having control of the structure, I now get to have control of the content. Here the prospect asks questions at the structural level, giving her control of the direction of the call. Let's look at this model again (see the illustration on the next page).

Where Do We Go from Here?

After I present and answer Martha's questions, I will ask my ultimate question: "Where do we go from here?" That question

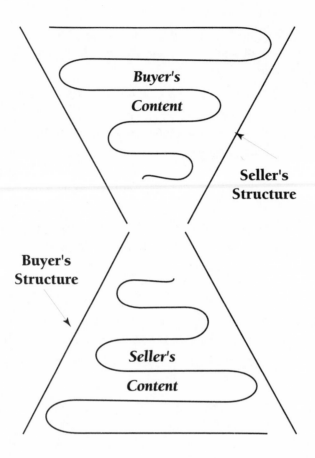

leads the prospect to her final brain scan—the search to see what else must happen. She's the one who moves the process forward, since it's her call. I will abide by her decision. I've done all I can do to serve her up to this point. If the seller pushes here, the rapport will be destroyed irreparably. The prospect will feel she has been led down the primrose path just to get the seller's needs met. She'll be right.

This is the Buying Facilitation process. It's quick. It's easy. *The most difficult part is getting out of the habit of trying to sell something.* And I don't say that lightly. That seems to be the only stumbling block for new facilitators.

The Thinking Process of Buying Facilitation

I'd like to go sequentially through the steps in my brain each time I approach a new prospect. It might help you to understand the considerations I go through.

1. I begin each call with a blank brain. If I have anything going on in my brain, any predetermined outcome for the call, any pitch I want to fit in, any opening commentary I'm thinking of, I am entering the call with a selling pattern and am not available to enter into a "We Space." I understand it is difficult to enter a call without an outcome, a goal in mind. I'd like you to consider this: your outcome is to *create an environment in which your prospect can have the support to discover how to get her needs met.* In a nutshell, your job is to create an environment in which you can serve. Your job is not to sell. To create that environment, you need a "We Space" and rapport. You can't have either if you have a prescribed outcome, which is dependent upon getting another person to do what you want her to do. Just enter, ask if it's a good time, and proceed—together.

2. In the beginning of the call, while I am figuring out how to enter the interaction sensitively and appropriately, I stay in *Neutral.* I let the information in without my brain taking over. Once the prospect begins to tell me about her environment, I switch to *Observer* so I can begin to make enough sense of what I'm hearing to know whether to formulate a question, agree, or summarize.

3. I move back and forth between *Self* and Observer during the remainder of the call. Because my "seller brain" is always wanting to step in and tell my prospect why she needs my product, I must stay in Observer and listen to what is being said. I make sure I'm curious, with the understanding that it's my job to help her help herself, since it is only when she realizes she can't that she will consider my product. The filter of "curiosity" rather than "sell" keeps me in line.

4. I provide tight parameters in which the conversation can take place. I do this by staying within the Funnel and continually formulating questions that make the prospect go inside for a search and go inside again. Her brain must find the information that will provide her with her values, her evidence, her problems, a defined problem space, her political considerations, and so on.

5. My brain is processing the information only insofar as is necessary to formulate the next question. When I hear the prospect patting herself on the back, I step out of questioning mode and agree. "That sounds great!" "I'm impressed." Agreement lets the prospect know that I am with her and on her team. I am.

6. After several parcels of information have been put forth, I summarize, mostly to make sure I'm on the right track and going down the Funnel in an effective manner. It also puts the prospect into Observer and gives her pause to reflect on what she's said.

7. I make a determination whether or not it appears we should be considering working together, based on a problem, if any, or the magnitude of the Problem Space. If it seems she is quite happy with her situation—*whether or not I think it needs to be fixed*—I say, "It sounds to me like you are doing really well using the system you've got in place. It doesn't seem you are needing anything different from what you have." When she agrees, we end the conversation. Only about 30 percent of the calls I make lead to a second call. The rest of the prospects are happy where they're at—or may call me later on if their system changes.

8. If your prospect is happy with her current supplier, and your product or service is not being addressed, it's okay to ask "Are there any conditions under which you would consider supplementing your current supplier?" Chances are she'd be willing to give you a shot if you've been respectful and responsible. *Don't ask a prospect to give up her current supplier for you. She has no reason to until she knows and trusts you and your product.*

9. Once the prospect is down the Funnel and we have both determined there may be a need that my product or service can fill, I go into Self and answer all the questions that apply to the prospect's environment. While I am out of control of the direction of the call at this point, I still must take the responsibility to maintain the collaboration. If at any point I begin addressing my own needs, I will potentially lose the connection.

10. I remain on the alert for shifts in the prospect's speaking style—language pattern, tone, volume. If I notice changes in speaking or language patterns (or gross body changes when face-to-face), I may have unwittingly stepped on her toes. I then question the prospect as to whether I've said something that she takes exception to. If I don't mention it, I can lose the collaboration. *Note that whenever the prospect exhibits major shifts in patterns, something has changed.* Remember that I am taking responsibility for the interaction here.

11. When I've finished addressing the information the prospect is interested in exploring, I begin to find out where we go from here. How will she know that what I have/do will support her need? Does she want references? How? Does she want information? What type? When? How does she want to receive it? Does she want another call? When? Who else needs to be on the line? Does she want a conference call? How about if I speak with some of the team members? Some of the other decision makers? Does she want me to visit? When? What is her time frame? How does she want me to support her in all this? How often should we speak? How can I support her with the team? What does she need to do to hold up her end? Does she need my support in any of that?

12. Once we end the call, I do everything I've agreed to: nothing more, nothing less. That includes call backs, visits, information, conference call. I also assume she'll do what she's promised. If she doesn't stick with her end of the bargain, I wait until a sufficient amount of time has passed and call *once*. I either speak to her directly (unlikely) or leave a voice mail saying that I am not sure where to go from here, but will wait until I hear from her before going forward. *You do not know what the culture, the Problem Space, the decision-making body is going through at this point. It's not your call. Trust the process. She will either be a client or not. You've done your job.*

As a seller, my favorite outcome of the process (besides increased revenue) is that prospects can figure out what they need—or not—and where, when, and how to proceed, if appropriate, on the first call. My lead time drops dramatically, and my sales cycle is diminished by at least half. I also know exactly what part of the decision-making cycle prospects are in so I can predict revenue.

As a servant, my favorite outcome of this process is that I get to assist people in discovering how they can get their own needs met effectively and efficiently, in a manner congruent with their values. I get to work interdependently, in a collaborative setting, with people offering respect, trust, and honesty to each other.

Win–win.

Chapter 13

Strengthening Customer Service through Buying Facilitation

Buying Facilitation uses the same model for customer service as it does for sales: the customer service representative (CSR) brings the customer down the Buying Decision Funnel, from where he is at to where he wants to be, exploring how to get there. The difference is that the questions are asked to support a customer's Problem Space and Solution Space rather than to discover a solution.

Currently, CSRs are trained to do the job of helping customers. That means they generally put task before relationship: here's how I can help, here's what we can and can't do, let me send you this. Often CSRs forget there are real people on the other end of the phone, people who are generally upset or angry. Putting task before relationship in this instance really doesn't serve the customer.

The one company I am familiar with that absolutely puts customers first is Nordstrom. I've heard that Nordstrom has a one-line customer service policy: "Use your best judgment." Whether that is true or not isn't the point. The point is that if people perpetuate that story there must be some truth behind it. Imagine if all customer service departments worked from that policy, trusting their staff to support customers in the best way for the customer.

In customer service, the most important thing is to let the customer know he has been heard and his feelings count. The CSR must also gather the information as to how specifically the customer wants his problem solved—angry customers always know how they want their problems solved *before they dial the phone to complain*—even if the CSR cannot solve it in that fashion.

The Customer Service Model

Let me go through a simple call to show how Buying Facilitation works in customer service.

CSR: "Hello. ABC Company. How can I help?"

CUS: "Hello. I'm calling with a complaint. Who do I speak with?"

1. CSR: "You sound *angry*. Tell me about it."

---

1. It is important to match the volume and tone of the customer's voice in order to be in rapport and to address the feeling head on. This alone will let the customer know he is being heard and will help him calm down. He is in *Self*. The CSR needs to be in *Observer* so as not to take any of this personally, as well as to have the full range of communication choices available to him.

CUS: "You *bet* I'm angry. Just this week, I bought those speakers you had on special, and they *still* cost me $500. They aren't working and I need them for my daughter's wedding on Saturday. I want your people to come by here and pick them up *tomorrow* and bring me the new ones at the same time so my daughter can have music at her wedding."

2. CSR: "So let me get this right. You bought our speakers and they're not working. I'm really sorry about that. You need them in two days. You want us to exchange them so you have speakers for your daughter's wedding. Did I get that right?"

---

2. The CSR is matching the customer's voice, summarizing the customer's solution, and building rapport within a "We Space." The client should feel heard.

CUS: "That's right. When can you come? I'll be home tomorrow afternoon."

3. CSR: "I hear that you want us to come tomorrow. Let me see what we can do. First of all, I'll need you to check out all the problems with our speaker specialist. I can have you do that in the next twenty minutes. I know your speakers aren't working, and we'll get you ones that do. We just need to know exactly what the problem is before proceeding. Is that okay?"

---

3. There are some housekeeping duties that must be performed, which the client might not like. So long as the CSR stays in rapport and lets the client know he is being heard, the CSR can get his job done. But he's got to be careful to always let the client know how important the complaint is.

CUS: "Does that mean you're not going to give me new speakers?"

4. CSR: "No. I just need to get some of the paperwork done here so we can proceed. I really hear that you need working speakers. How would it be if the technical person could actually find a way to make the speakers work? Would you be willing to keep them?"

---

4. Rapport, rapport, rapport. Since it is possible that there is nothing wrong with the speakers, the CSR must set the stage for all the possibilities up front.

CUS: "As long as they work for the wedding. But if that doesn't work, are you going to replace them?"

5. CSR: "Yes, we will. I want you to have speakers for your daughter's wedding also. Since I need you to speak with a technical person, and we need to speak again following that call, how do you want to proceed? Do you want me to call you back? Do you want to call me back?"

---

5. The customer must know that he is in control, but the CSR keeps control at the structural level, just like in the sales call: win-win or no deal, seller/CSR in control of the structure, customer in control of the content.

CUS: "Have him call me. Then I'll call you back after I have spoken with him. If there's a problem—and those speakers still are not working—can you promise me I'll have speakers by Saturday?"

CSR: "I promise you will have your speakers for Saturday. Thank you for your patience, and sorry you've had to go through this trouble. I hope the speakers will work well for you. They're a great product. And let me know if there is anything else I can do."

The "We Space" is apparent in the above example. And no matter what happens in this situation (as long as the speakers are replaced on time), that company has a loyal customer.

When I field a customer service call, I go through the same process of blanking my brain and working from Observer that I do in a sales call. In fact, the principles, beliefs, and skills are identical—only the content shifts.

Using *Observer* to Remain in Equilibrium

Working from Observer is the key to a good customer service call. Too often customer service reps get into Self when dealing with an angry customer who is screaming or demanding. While teaching customer service classes, the biggest complaint I get is that reps don't want to be talked to "like that" and that customers have "no right" to be so rude. In fact, customers are in Self and are not aware they are speaking so loudly or rudely. If the reps are in Self also, it feels like customers are screaming at them, personally. Once the reps learn to sit back and go into Observer, they are no longer in the loop and are able to see the situation with more clarity.

I recommend an additional behavioral approach that CSRs can use to help customers calm down when they are loud and rude. I know it runs counter to everything that is taught about customer service, so please try it before rejecting it. It has worked for countless customer service groups I have taught.

If you want to calm the customer down *match your voice* to his. Yes, be loud if he is loud. Clipped if his voice is clipped. You need not sound angry—just loud or clipped. You can deliver your normal response using the words you would normally use—just louder.

Have you ever had an argument with a person who was very excited and you were calm? What happened? Your communication partner probably got more upset as you stayed calm because you were out of rapport! People only notice differences, and if you are calm when your customer is flustered, you are out of rapport. If you match your voice to your customer's voice, *he will not notice your voice being loud; he will experience rapport.*

I am not saying to scream back. I am saying to use a loud voice with your words. "I hear you are angry" can be spoken in any voice tone. I recommend you use the same voice tone your angry customer uses. You will not have to maintain that level for too long—not usually for more than a sentence or two. But the very act of getting into voice rapport will help ensure that your customer will feel heard and calm down quickly. After all, he knows you are not at fault and are just a representative of the company. His intent is not to annoy you, and by being in rapport with him you will be serving him.

One more point about customer service calls: it is estimated that 60 percent of customers with a problem never bother to complain. The 40 percent who do call are probably your most loyal customers (or they wouldn't bother calling). Therefore, a customer service call has within it the potential for additional business. As you get into more rapport during the conversation, and as you are assisting your customer through the problem, begin to ask Buying Decision Funnel questions. Not that you want to sell something now—you want to concentrate on the problem being solved. But there might be instances in which your questions would lead to future conversations to handle additional needs. Use your judgment as to whether it's appropriate or not.

Chapter 14

Case Comparisons: Buying Facilitation, Traditional Sales, and Consultative Sales

To give you a more complete feel for how Buying Facilitation works, I've put forth three case histories—one for Traditional sales, one for Consultative sales, and one for Buying Facilitation. I go through the same mom-and-pop construction environment to show the differences in the methodologies. I will introduce the scenario by using the decision-making strategy so you will be aware of all the aspects of the Problem Space. Then you can see how each sales approach deals with the problem, the Problem Space, the solution, and the Solution Space. While many of you sell in situations different from this, I believe you will be able to translate the skills.

Background

Don & Son (D&S) is a small, successful construction company and has been family run since its inception thirty years ago. Once owned by Don, it is now owned by his son, Jim. Don has given the business to Jim but continues to work there daily. Father and son enjoy each other's company and actually work well together. But Don will be retiring in the near future.

187

Funnel Information

1. Look at the entire environment as it is in the present.

Jim likes and respects Don, his father, and wants to keep his expertise around. Don's formal role is to do the accounting for the firm. He keeps an informal eye on the progression of the work at the sites and the materials flow.

2. Look at where the company is going in the near and intermediate future.

Jim is looking to grow the company. He's just hiring a new architect and believes he should be in a good position to get some of those fancier jobs he's not gone after so far.

3. Notice if all the components are in place to bring the company through to the future vision.

Jim is not sure what he'll need to grow. He guesses there will be some additional time demands on him. After meeting with his team and discussing his ideas about growing, a few areas have become obvious potential problem spots that could hinder growth: (1) He would need more cash flow to cover increased material costs. (2) There would be more material to track, which would mean more people to hire and pay, more site management issues. (3) Jim is beginning to notice that his dad's work is slowing down; so far Jim has been working around that problem.

4. If a missing piece would prevent the company from getting to the future vision, the missing piece must be found and added.

Jim thinks he can handle the potential cash flow problems by asking for a higher percentage of a job's costs up front. He doesn't think he has the ability to track more materials or keep up with the increased workload created by additional personnel, unless there is a shift in staffing patterns and requirements.

5. Look around the environment again. Talk with the team and collaboratively search for ways to use current internal resources to supply the missing piece.

Jim and his dad meet to discuss the possibility of Don covering the potential increased workload. Don is hoping to retire soon. He doesn't want to put in any more time than he is now, and may begin working even fewer hours. He's certain, however, that he wants to keep his hand in somehow. Jim speaks with the rest of the team to discuss the possibility of some of them taking on extra work. There doesn't seem to be any extra time they can devote.

6. *If there are no internal resources to fix the problem, prepare to look externally for resources to supply the missing piece. Get team agreement and feedback as to how to proceed.*

It seems Don will not be able to take on extra work. The other team members don't have extra time. Jim is either going to have to do the additional work himself or bring in something or someone to pick up the slack. The company has been doing well, and everyone is working happily together, so it's not a clear decision whether or not to upset the apple cart and do something different. It's important to Jim to be able to grow while keeping his people happy and the organization healthy. He has another team meeting. All are in agreement with some type of external resource being brought in to solve the problem as long as there is adequate time given to decision making, planning, integration, and problem solving. In fact, Jim's been hearing his colleagues talk about computer software that handles all the day-to-day problems and frees up personnel to take on more work and be more creative.

7. *Determine with the team the criteria to be used to locate, choose, and integrate the missing piece. Look at the systemic issues to identify criteria (i.e., people and staffing needs, internal politics, timing, budget, outcome).*

After speaking with several other contractors at an annual convention, Jim decides to look at some software packages to track his material handling and do his accounting. He is interested in packages that are easy to learn and use, and efficient enough that he won't need to bring new people into the company. He has a flexible budget to a point, and if he can get exactly what he wants he's willing to pay the price. He wants to make sure the team decides together, since they're the ones who will be using the package. And most of all, he wants to make sure his dad can learn the software quickly and use it easily. In fact, his dad gets two votes on the ultimate choice.

8. *Authorize team members to search for the missing piece by exploring potential external resources using the chosen criteria as a filter for choice.*

Jim has heard of several software packages that will do what he needs done on the accounting side, the tracking side, and the people side. He decides to have his secretary, Sara, call and gather the information he'll need to make a decision.

9. *Find several potential fixes. Bring possibilities back to the environment and entire team to get consensus as to the best choice.*

Over the next month, Sara brings back lots of information. The team sits down to discuss the options and decide where they want to go with the information at hand. They have strong preferences for two of the options and decide to seek further information from the salespeople on these two, as well as have an in-house demonstration so they can all see how the package works. Once they have the information that will show them how the package will meet their job needs, their people needs in general, and specifically the need to have Don be happy with the system, they'll be able to make a decision.

10. *Bring in the external fix; integrate it into the existing environment.*

They choose the package. Don was given the final vote, and he's actually looking forward to learning the new technology and seeing the company expand in this new direction. Now the interesting part begins: dealing with the learning curve, the effect on the team, and the effect on job descriptions.

The new software gives Jim the ability to grow his company into the future according to his vision, as well as expand the skills his people have. And Jim also has his dad right there next to him, learning, growing, and overseeing—just as it should be.

Case Histories

Traditional Sales—The Seller's Story

Pam sells a construction software package. She begins calling construction sites to see which ones would be interested in a face-to-face meeting to discuss the product. Pam gets an appointment with Don & Son and comes in to meet with Sara to present the product. It is obvious to Pam, after doing her homework and doing research on the firm, that D&S needs the package. She studies hard for her presentation. Once she arrives at D&S, she realizes she is only meeting with Sara, who is obviously not the decision maker. She tries to get Sara to bring in the boss, but to no avail. Because she's meeting with such a junior person Pam thinks she is being given the runaround, so she tries harder to present all of the functions of the package that will obviously help D&S grow. She leaves with the promise that someone will get back to her within the next month. Pam doesn't believe it, and when she doesn't hear back within a week, Pam starts calling to find out what's happening and also to attempt to speak with the owner. Sara gets more and more annoyed with Pam's calls, but the product is good so she tells her to please wait and Sara will call her back. Pam continues to call, trying to make friends with Sara. Eventually, Sara is so annoyed with Pam that she takes her out of the loop as Sara doesn't want to have to deal with Pam on a continuing basis.

Consultative Sales—The Seller's Story

Pam is selling a software construction package and finds Don & Son to be a qualified prospect. She gets an appointment to meet with Sara, and sits down with her to discuss her needs, letting her know clearly that Pam's intent is to collaborate with her. What is D&S looking for? What is their environment like? How do they want to grow? What is stopping them from being all they can be? Sara answers the questions and forms a comfortable relationship with Pam. Once Sara is finished answering questions and sharing information, Pam presents her product, careful to address each one of Sara's needs. Pam stresses the sophistication of the package and discusses the learning curve. Yes, it's steep, but then again it offers all that Sara needs to help the company grow. It's even priced competitively. Then Pam recommends which parts of the package Sara should be looking at purchasing in accordance with the stated needs for growth. She sets up a follow-up schedule with Sara to possibly demonstrate the package to the owner. Pam leaves Sara with lots of written material and a date to connect within the month. Given their relationship and the way the product fits into the future plans of the company—and the success of the sales call—Pam gives the sale an 80 percent chance of moving forward to a close. She follows up with Sara, and ultimately Sara tells her that the product is a bit too sophisticated for their needs. Pam is very surprised at the lost sale.

Buying Facilitation—The Seller's Story

Pam is a seller of a software construction package. She places a phone call to Don & Son, and after getting into rapport, she asks the person she is speaking with if there is a need in that company for a software package that will handle accounting and site management. Sara is delighted to speak with Pam. With Sara's permission, Pam begins asking questions about the present environment. Sara can answer only some of these questions, and as the questions get more complex, she needs help answering them. She grabs Jim to get on the line with her.

- How are accounting and site management being handled now?
- Who is doing it?
- You are successful. Are there any reasons you would want to change what you are doing?
- What would you be doing differently if you were getting all your needs met? What's stopping you from doing all of that right now?
- What resources do you have internally to help you in getting where you want to be? What's stopping you from using those resources?
- If you don't have appropriate resources to get you where

you'd like to be, how would you make a decision to look for or bring in an external resource?

■ What criteria would you use in choosing a software package?

■ How would you know that my product would suit your needs?

■ How would you like me to proceed?

Since Jim has already decided he cannot meet his needs internally, he tells Pam he needs written material, then references to examine the ease of use to make sure Don can learn quickly and easily. If those things line up, Jim would like Pam to come in and do a demo with the team. Pam suggests to Jim that once he gets the information from her, he sit down with Don and go over the material and write down all of his questions. Then, when Jim calls the references he can make sure Don's issues get addressed. She also offers to speak with Don if Don isn't sure what all of his questions are. Pam tells Jim that there are specific segments of the software that are more complex than others, and that if those specific pieces are the ones Don would be using most frequently, this may not be the package for them and she could recommend others that have more ease of use.

Pam and Jim end with a date in two weeks to have a discussion of whether or not the material and references and Don's comfort level suggest that the package is appropriate. If so, Jim would want Pam to come in four weeks later to give a demo to the entire staff. He also asks to pass her number along to Don, so Don can ask her questions independently. Pam has no idea whether she will make a sale here, since it is dependent upon whether this package will meet Don's needs or another product would suit Jim and Don better.

That's the complete process. Notice how Pam's behaviors, goals, expectations, and outcomes differ in all of the approaches. Notice how different the interaction is when the goal is to serve.

Before going into the daily activities involved in working with Buying Facilitation, I will spend some time in the next chapter on the issue of managing in a Buying Facilitation environment.

SKILL SET #15:

The Buying Facilitation Method

Write down all of the elements of Buying Facilitation, putting those that you find the most comfortable first, and those that make you least comfortable last.

- [ ] Begin to work with each element, one at a time.

- [ ] Keep a learning journal. Note which elements make you uncomfortable and why. Note what happens with the discomfort. Work with Self and Observer to make it easier. What happens when you shift your position? Do your choices increase?

- [ ] Notice the differences in the reactions you get from prospects and clients when using elements of Buying Facilitation. Notice the similarities also.

- [ ] Remember that you have a learning curve. Notice what elements are harder for you to learn than others. Why is this so? How can you push your way through this?

- [ ] Think about and write down specifics (in the areas of skills, beliefs, behaviors, the questioning process, the listening process, and so on) of what you need to know to be comfortable enough with the process and with your potential learning curve to push through to the levels of learning and unlearning necessary to take on the new methodology.

- [ ] How will you know it is worthwhile learning?

- [ ] What skills and behaviors are you currently using that will be necessary to alter or give up? How do you plan to do that?

Chapter 15

Managing Salespeople in a Buying Facilitation Environment

When Buying Facilitation is being used in a sales environment, closing is not the focus. Because Buying Facilitation is based on the belief that people buy when and what they need, sellers don't need to "close" at all: buyer and seller know together when it is appropriate to buy. Sellers will be wasting little time on inappropriate prospects, and appropriate ones know how to buy much, much faster.

Managing the Belief Change

More than anything, Buying Facilitation brings a change in direction into the sales environment. It announces that the company backs a principle-centered sales force, a sales force whose goal is service and whose focus is not to make a sale but to facilitate the buyer.

Recently, I was asked to train an entire inside sales force of one of the largest companies in America. I told them I would love to, on one condition: the entire company would have to support a belief change and become a service-oriented rather than product-oriented company. They agreed. But had they not, it would have been very difficult to expect the sales reps to work from a service base while the rest of the work environment was product oriented. The company would have had a solution much smaller than the Problem Space, with no way for the sales reps to get support.

Imagine if the sales team were using Buying Facilitation and the sales manager asked them to do a cold-calling blitz for one week on purchased leads to sell one specific product. It would go against everything Buying Facilitation stands for and would compromise the sellers.

If there is a true understanding that people only buy what they need, when they need it, and how they need it, a cold-calling blitz would be incongruent since it works on a numbers game model: make enough calls and you can find enough people who will buy the product. A blitz does not respect either buyer or seller. Sure, it "works" and brings in revenue if there are enough sellers placing enough calls. But if those same sellers used those same leads to discover actual needs, how much *more* revenue might have been discovered—not to mention loyal customers created.

It's Okay Not to Sell

The biggest belief change required to implement Buying Facilitation is that it is okay not to sell a product if it would be an inappropriate decision for the prospect. This idea goes against most companies' sales efforts.

I received a call from a salesperson using Buying Facilitation. He told me that he had gone down the Funnel with a new prospect and between them they discovered that the seller's product would be inappropriate for the prospect's needs. When asked by his sales manager what had happened on the call, the seller related the details, stating he had deleted the prospect from his active files. The manager was furious, telling him it was his job to convince the prospect, whether the prospect needed the product or not.

In this case, again, the new sales approach did not fit in with the company's values: the sales manager and seller were working out of two different sets of beliefs.

But How Can We Forecast and Meet Quotas?

Here are some answers to questions I commonly hear from sales managers:

Q: Will the company be able to forecast? Will the sellers be able to?

A: Forecasting is much easier with Buying Facilitation. Only qualified leads are in the pipeline, and sellers and buyers collaborate to decide how to go forward. There are no more "sellers' voids" in which sellers can only guess what will happen, when.

Q: How do we know if the sellers will meet the quotas we need them to meet to keep our business afloat?

A: Quotas, as they are currently set, support the numbers game: make enough calls and you'll make your quota. When time is spent only on prospecting or supporting qualified prospects, sales should increase dramatically.

Q: Will we sell *anything* with all this relationship stuff?

A: Relationship will enhance the discovery process. Prospects will have higher quality information sooner as a result of the seller's questions, and appropriate prospects will become buyers sooner than before.

Q: How do I support my sellers if I don't have the same questioning skills they use? What skills will I need to help them? And how do I get those skills?

A: Sales management focuses on supporting communication skills, such as

- formulating questions;
- creating rapport, trust, and collaboration;
- taking responsibility to communicate effectively;

■ learning to stay in Observer;

■ learning to listen and deliver feedback;

■ maintaining and creating relationships;

■ understanding the prospect's meta-messages;

■ learning to recognize early on when there is a fit and when to throw the number away.

Managers must study the skills of Buying Facilitation along with sellers, but they won't have all the skills right away. For companies with more than one sales team, managers can do peer coaching to support each other in learning the skills.

Q: How will I know when my staff needs help? How will I know when they're in trouble?

A: When managers sit with their sellers and notice them using selling patterns *and* notice they are not meeting quotas, managers will have to assist sellers in improving their skills.

What Skills Do Sales Managers Need?

Make no mistake: the skill set required for Buying Facilitation is *very different*. Sellers must learn to formulate appropriate questions, and this takes time and practice.

In the most successful Buying Facilitation environments I've visited, the sales managers sit with their sales staff several hours a day and listen to their calls in order to help sellers with their skills. They sit behind one seller at a time for fifteen minutes or so and take notes on what they hear. They listen for

■ rapport;

■ questioning skills;

■ ability to move between Self and Observer;

■ ability to move between summarizing, questioning, and agreeing;

■ ability to move down the Funnel appropriately—not too quickly (which leaves out vital information) or too slowly (which stays in content and doesn't end the conversation with decisions and possible action items).

Because the goal of Buying Facilitation is to serve and the outcome is discovery, the seller must learn to formulate and use questions very differently than he is used to. A facilitated call can quickly become a manipulative call with the wrong questions. Because the purchase of a product grows out of service, sellers must maintain their curiosity and desire to serve even when they believe they can help the prospect buy by offering just the right answers or advice.

Teaching Teams

Buying Facilitation works best when sales managers supervise their sellers in teams of about four people. Each team should meet weekly and share their best and worst calls of the week. They can do this by keeping a record each day of their best and worst calls, and then, at the end of the week, deciding on their best and worst for the week. Sellers should also tape one hour of their calls every day for the first two months they are learning Buying Facilitation. They can listen to the tapes while driving to and from work, and report their progress weekly along with their best and worst call discussions.

Asking sellers to assume this level of activity to learn the new skill set will do several things. First, it will take the sting out of mistakes; everyone will be able to laugh with and support each other. Sellers will also learn from each other's mistakes and successes. Secondly and most important, it will let the sellers know that the company is supporting the new method and putting time and staff behind it. It is difficult for sellers to learn Buying Facilitation without support from management as there is nowhere to practice except at work, and when they are practicing, they are going against what's expected from them and their peers.

What Will the New Sales Environment Look Like?

In a sales environment where the principles of Buying Facilitation have been adopted, the right buyers will be found sooner, given that the company has adequate and appropriate leads.

The routine I recommend is to use the phone to place qualifying calls and find interested prospects. I advise two cold-calling sessions of two hours each, three days a week (for a total of twelve hours), if possible. This can generate at least thirty contacts a day, with about five qualified prospects. At three days a week, over the course of a month, there will be about sixty qualified prospects. Two days a week, the sellers go to the field to visit these people, leaving only a few hours a week for administrative tasks. Environments using Buying Facilitation find they need more administrative staff to support the additional work generated by the increased number of qualified prospects.

The efficiency of only working with and visiting qualified prospects will lead to more prospecting time on the phone. Given the expanded time frame, the Buying Facilitation method can be used for "hello" calls (to make contact and check in) and follow-up calls. Since there is increased contact with clients as well as prospects, sellers end up with mountains of paperwork to support the regular client base. This work was there all along, of course, but the issues never got dealt with because there was less client contact.

For those sellers who believe they need to get in front of a prospect to make a sale, I suggest they just go to see those who are ready to buy and not use visits to do the qualifying. With the time saved by not going to the field to qualify, they'll have more time for prospecting and maintaining their current client base.

To summarize, in Buying Facilitation environments:

There will be more phone time for qualifying prospects.

There will be more administrative work to be done with the increase in contacts.

What Happens When Buying Facilitation Is Being Used Incompletely?

Following are some standard objections that prospects use:

- "There's no money; it's too expensive."
- "I'm not the decision maker."
- "We're going to have to wait another six months until:
  ... the reorganization ... the downsizing or the right-sizing."
- "We've changed our minds."
- "We're not sure yet what we need."
- "The competitive product is cheaper and is good enough."
- "We don't have any needs, thank you."
- "We'll call you back when we're ready."

Following are some objections prospects use when not returning a seller's calls:

- "Nobody has had a chance to look at the material."
- "The decision maker is out for two weeks on unexpected business."
- Or the seller may keep getting the prospect's voice mail when a decision is expected.

When the seller hears these objections, he has not used the Buying Facilitation method correctly. The prospect is feeling in an adversarial position and that the seller is attempting to get his own needs met *at the expense of the prospect*.

It is hard to believe it until you try it, but when sellers use Buying Facilitation, they get no objections. Prospects have nothing to object to when a seller is supporting their discovery. Issues like money, decision making, and return calls are all worked out during the questioning process, and both prospect and seller have a hand in working out whatever has come up.

Money Objections

The classic objection, money, is merely a case of a prospect saying "no" in the most expedient way. Money is rarely the reason people don't purchase a product. Unless they are a small company, most budgets have some flexibility—spreading out payments, using financing, "borrowing" from another budgeted purchase. I'll never forget a comment one of my prospects made after objecting to my price and receiving a surprising response:

"I am expensive. That's true," I said.

"Hmm. I guess we're going to have to find the money somewhere."

If sellers are getting price objections regularly, it might be that they are making some attempt to convince or persuade.

"Closing" the Sale

Traditionally, sellers use techniques to get a prospect to make some sort of commitment on how to proceed. In Buying Facilitation, that is not necessary. By the time the questioning process is complete, prospects will know exactly what needs to be done. If there is a match between the prospect's need to buy and the seller's product, the prospect will have a list of next steps. In the mom-and-pop construction company software purchase scenario in the last chapter, for example, Jim knew he had to meet with Don to go over the material Pam would send, ask Don to formulate his questions, and give Pam's phone number to Don.

The final question, "Where do we go from here?" creates the need for the prospect to summarize his immediate next steps as well as all the actions necessary for him to follow up. Remember: *Service is the goal; discovery is the outcome; a sale may be the solution.* There is no need for the seller to force a commitment from a prospect; it will be obvious.

It will also be obvious if the appropriate action is to end the call with a simple "Thank you for your time" or with a request for referrals. In either case, the seller does not keep the prospect in the pipeline and does not need to follow up.

Managing the Sales Cycle

When running a team using Buying Facilitation, sales managers must understand there is a different sales cycle and different expectations of how the sale will proceed.

First of all, a seller should be able to qualify prospects in one call—two maximum. Then a seller follows up according to how the prospect wants follow-up—*not according to how the seller wants to follow up*. If the prospect wants written information or to speak with references rather than to meet the seller face-to-face, that's the way the follow-up is carried out. Therefore, managers can't determine how a sale is proceeding based on numbers of visits.

Another aspect of the sales environment that is different for sellers using Buying Facilitation is the fact that *each person who is spoken with is a prospect.* Many teams I visit do not count the receptionist or secretary as a contact, even though she can strongly influence the process. Since there is so much information exchanged with whomever answers the phone, each contact counts. I will discuss this more completely in the next chapter.

SKILL SET #16:

Managing the Buying Facilitation Environment

☐ What is your current belief around supervising sellers? What are your current outcomes? What skills do you use to support your beliefs and outcomes?

☐ How do your current supervision skills support your personal and team values and ethics? Do those differ from your company values and ethics? If so, what needs to happen to get them aligned?

☐ What would need to happen for you to supervise your team using Buying Facilitation in a way that would support the company, the team, the prospect, the clients, and you? How would you go about implementing that? What would have to happen?

☐ What, if anything, would stop you from gaining the skills and support to supervise a team using Buying Facilitation? How would you start? What would you need to know or do differently to learn the skills needed for this type of sales/supervision? How would you begin that?

☐ How would you know it's time to bring Buying Facilitation into your team? How would your team decide this?

Chapter 16

Buying Facilitation in Action
On-the-Phone, Face-to-Face, and Across Sales Contexts

Now that you are aware of all the pieces of Buying Facilitation, I'd like to explore how this methodology will manifest itself in your daily selling. You will find many of your routine communications and professional expectations to be different, so I'll give you some idea of the changes to expect.

When to Use Buying Facilitation

The answer is simple: any time a prospect may have a need that your product or service will meet. This includes large items and small, face-to-face sales and telesales, telemarketing and consulting. The method is not industry specific since we're not working on the content level, and it is not reserved for prospecting, customer service, or sales. In fact, you may find yourself using this communication approach with all types of people and situations, from teenagers ("What are you doing right now in the way of dealing with your commitment to school?" "Are there any conditions under which you would consider keeping your room neat?") to car mechanics ("I've got an emergency repair I need done and I bet you're really busy. What would need to happen for you to be able to sneak me in today?")

Any time you have a client, a friend, a prospect, a family member who may need additional service or support, go right into the Funnel. Remember that your questions will help people help themselves and expand their understanding of their Problem Space and Solution Space. The people you support will also bring you increased business when appropriate.

What to Expect in the Buying Facilitation Process

The Sales Cycle

One of the reasons a sales cycle takes the time it takes is because prospects are figuring out how to make sense of their environment in a culturally responsible way. Your use of the Buying Decision Funnel will bring the issues forward and your sales cycle should be cut in half. The cycle will include the following:

1. Rapport and discovery, product description as appropriate;

2. Follow-up, with information or demonstration when appropriate;

3. Support and close/complete.

Getting to the Right Person

Sellers often have been given a name and number to call from a previous seller's records, a lead-generating program, or some other source. Often these names are inappropriate for many reasons, and you only find that out after two months of trying to make contact. When you call the number, ask the person who answers, "Could you tell me who'd be the best person to speak with for information regarding your managment training needs?" Given the rapport you will have built (remember that everyone who answers the phone is your prospect), you'll get the right name the first time. If you are stuck, ask for the secretary or assistant to the chief decision maker, tell her your line of business, and ask her who she recommends you speak with.

When you go in looking for the CEO or president, the odds are slim to none that you will (1) get through, and/or (2) make a sale without this person delegating the decision back to the appropriate department. You are just wasting time. Trust that your questions will bring the appropriate people into the decision. Just get to the best person first.

Opening Statements

When you open with a great line or hard-to-ignore statement, you are manipulating, not to mention making the statement into a void. Nobody is listening. Don't waste your breath or the vital first few moments when you could be getting into rapport and setting up a "We Space." One more thing: in real life, people who are in rapport do not use each other's names frequently. Although Dale Carnegie suggested you use the person's name to let her know you are in rapport, the opposite is true. The same with asking after someone's health. Everyone who responds to a stranger when asked how they are says "fine." This starts the conversation out with a lie.

Pitches

You've been used to pitches; now you won't need one until the prospect has discovered exactly what she needs. Then, when it's the appropriate time to go into content, address the issues the prospect has discovered as part of her criteria for bringing in an external solution. Nothing more, nothing less. Sure, your product or service can do much more than the prospect wants to hear about. In time, with a fuller relationship, you might get the chance to enlighten her. But once she's decided what she wants to buy and how, you'd be severely out of rapport if you tried to push your product. Besides, it violates all the principles of Buying Facilitation. Don't forget to answer the prospect's early curiosity with extremely brief responses. That's all she needs until she is ready and able to hear and understand it all.

Objections

There is nothing to object to. You are supporting a prospect's decisions. People only object when they have to defend against a seller who is attempting to get her own needs met rather than the prospect's needs.

Closes

I know that many sales approaches use closing techniques as a way to maneuver a prospect into an agreement or commitment to purchase. But since *you can't make a sale without a buyer,* it's the prospect's call as to how to move forward. Only one of two things can happen at the end of the Buying Facilitation process: you and your prospect decide to end your association, or you decide to move forward. If your product is considered a viable solution, the prospect will know how she must proceed given the parameters of how decisions get made in her company.

I recommend a one-line close to respect the prospect's position: "Where do we go from here?" If the result of the discovery process is to move ahead, the prospect will answer you with her favorite buying patterns. If she should ask you to send material, for example, ask her specifically what material would give her the information she needs. In this instance, it is not a put-off but a way of buying through a visual channel. Remember to respect her needs and don't push for what you would consider a commitment. Trust that you've gone down the Funnel together, and are concluding appropriately.

Rejections

I wish I could tell you that you will no longer be rejected. Sales has had such a bad reputation for so long that there is a small percentage of people who will reject you just because you are a sales-person. But if you get into rapport quickly and establish a basis of trust, the amount of rejection directed at you will be minimal. If you are finding a high degree of rejection while using Buying Facil-itation, check out your rapport-building skills and tape yourself to get a better idea of what you are doing. When you are making a call using a high level of rapport, the vast majority of the people you call will be friendly and eager to speak with you, even on a cold call. They will notice the difference in your approach imme-diately, and often even comment on it.

Screens

A screen—sometimes defined as the gatekeeper—has two functions: keep out inappropriate calls and let in appropriate ones. For some reason, sellers have forgotten the second one. A screen is your buyer, your receiver. In an interaction with a screen, who has the control? It's not you. If she believes that what you have is what her boss needs, you'll get through. I've had screens book appointments for their bosses with me—leading to large corporate jobs—when I've called on a cold call. I had one woman go into the men's room to find her boss to come speak with me. Another screen asked me for my material and took it around herself and closed the sale for me. Once I was even told that the boss was usu-ally drunk in the afternoons so calling in the morning would be more productive.

I use the same opening with the screen as I do with my other prospects. I ask if it's a good time to speak, tell her what my prod-uct is, and ask her how the company is handling whatever issues my product supports. In other words, I start going down the Fun-nel with her. She gets to decide what to do. It's her call. It was her call all along. Any seller who thinks that because she sounds important, or sounds like she knows the boss, she will be let through is mistaken. My secretary used to put messages from the people she didn't like at the bottom of my pile—and she would keep moving them to the bottom, not to be found for months. If she liked the person, she'd hound me until I returned the call. The screen really is your ally. She'll do as much to help you get business as anyone else in that company. Just get into a "We Space" with her.

Scripts

When you use a script, you are using a seller-based, product-specific methodology based on a numbers game: call enough people and you'll find one with buying patterns the same as the selling patterns in your script. Not only do you make a tiny percentage of sales under these conditions, but the seller as well as the prospect is being abused and disrespected. Learning the Funnel is easy—much easier than creating, learning, and delivering scripts that don't work.

Proposals

Proposals are a great way for prospects to get help organizing their thinking. They take proposals from several prospective vendors and use the information to help them think about their problem sequentially. Get the point? The ratio of written proposals to signed business is usually 10:1. With your questions and the Buying Decision Funnel you will know exactly which proposal to write, and will not have to bother with the other nine. Work on the real need for a proposal with your prospect. Sometimes you can alleviate the need for one if you just ask, "Are there any conditions under which you would consider working with me without a proposal?" If it's a nongovernment company, you can often get away without one.

Follow-up Calls

In the older sales methodologies, a high percentage of first calls ended right there, with the prospect not returning seller's calls—and calls, and calls. With Buying Facilitation, the prospect tells the seller how she wants her to follow up and is much more accessible to the seller since they are in partnership. If I have made an agreement regarding follow-up and it doesn't happen as planned, I leave a voice mail saying, "Hi. It's Sharon Drew. This was our arranged time and you must be busy. Call me when you want to proceed. Hope all is well."

The prospect probably had something come up, or the team took a different direction, or it's not the right timing. Sure, the nice thing would be for the prospect to call and let you know there's been a change—which does happen. Usually the prospect has forgotten or is embarrassed. She will call you when it's more appropriate—*or not*. Placing several calls will not change her readiness or the issues. If you had good rapport and went down the Funnel effectively without pushing or using your sales patterns, she will call you back when the time is right. You need to trust her as much as she trusts you. Remember, **there's no sale without a buyer.** By leading a prospect through the Funnel and supporting her in supporting herself, you've done your job. If she wants to close, she'll call; she's got your number. You can't close without her.

Voice Mail

I love voice mail. I get to ask lots of questions, bring my personality and beliefs to the party, and have an intimate connection— and the prospect gets to listen. My monologue sounds something like this:

> "Hi. My name is Sharon Drew Morgen and I was going to ask you if it was a good time to speak—but obviously it's not. This is a sales call. I sell a new brand of sales training based on ethics and values and collaboration. I was wondering what you were doing about bringing in new sales methodologies to your company, and how you would know if what I'm doing would fit your company culture and your sales team's needs. If you have needs or interest, please call me at . . ."

If you just leave a message asking a stranger to call you, she won't, unless she knows enough to know she needs you or your product specifically. When you haven't connected with someone already, leaving a sales pitch or a name with a request for a call back, and hoping you'll get one, is like planting a seed in a rock and hoping for a flower. In all likelihood it won't happen.

Call-Ins

When people call in with questions about your product, it's a perfect opportunity to begin going down the Funnel. The questions are usually content specific because the callers have recognized a problem and are gathering information for a solution. Often they haven't perceived all the implications of a new resource in their current environment. If you can facilitate them through the Buying Decision Funnel, they will get a clearer look at their Problem Space and their criteria for choosing an external resource. Reps who handle phone lines should be trained in Buying Facilitation in order to support discovery here.

Returned Mailers

Direct marketing teams do huge mailings, resulting in hundreds, if not thousands, of response cards. Often, subsidiary staff send in the responses for their bosses and put their bosses' names on the card. Sometimes, one team member is gathering information for the team. These response cards are letting you know that a team is in a decision-making process. Call the number and get into rapport with whoever answers. Tell her your company name and that you have received a request for information in the area of X. Ask her who she would recommend you speak with concerning the information requested. At least 50 percent of the time you will be put through to one of the members of the decision-making team, not necessarily the name listed on the card. Tell the person you reach that you have received a mailer requesting information from the person whose name is on the card, and then begin the Buying Facilitation process.

Frequently reps call and call and call for the person named on the card, and when they finally reach her, she wants them to speak with someone else. Sellers lose about two months in a sales cycle this way. Also, *don't ask if she has received any information already sent.* She may eventually mention it if she's read it, or ignore it if she hasn't. But this directs the call around a mailing piece rather than using the time for information support.

Appointments

The old model of task-oriented relationships held the belief that if a seller could get in front of a prospect, it would be easier to make a sale. How silly! Just because you are in front of someone means she'll have a greater need to buy from you??

A prospect either needs to purchase an external resource or not, is ready to bring in an external solution or not. Using the Buying Decision Funnel and your goal to serve, you can create a trust-based relationship on the phone and decide with your prospect whether or not you should be moving forward toward a sale. If your prospect wants to see you as part of her buying pattern, that's when you make an appointment. When you try to get an appointment as part of your selling pattern, you will only sell to those people who buy when they see a seller face-to-face. Conversely, you will leave out all those people who might need your product but who don't buy that way.

Presentations

I know this will sound strange to you and far out of your belief system, but I have made three presentations in my entire sales career. I know that some product lines demand one, but not so many as are being made. I would guess that something like 50 percent of all presentations are unnecessary. A presentation is like an opening or a pitch: it's a sender with no receiver, and the seller has no idea what the prospect needs or what the Problem Space looks like. Most presentations are based on solving a problem; they ignore the Space the problem is situated in.

If you believe you need to make a presentation (like proposals, prospects often ask for them to help themselves decide what it is they need), spend lots of phone time if possible getting at the prospect's specific needs and cultural issues. Then spend the first portion of your visit asking more questions and going down the Funnel. Once you and your prospect's team understand exactly what's needed, you can offer your presentation and "customize" it on the spot.

Industry-Specific Issues in Buying Facilitation

There are many types of selling situations and environments. Let's look at some specific industries to see how buying facilitation affects them.

Insurance

The insurance industry is one of the last bastions of the in-your-face sales approach. Brokers and agents still cold call for appointments. Over 80 percent of an insurance broker's time is spent in the field with inappropriate "suspects." Using Buying Facilitation will give insurance sellers 80 percent more time to be on the phone to find appropriate prospects and to service existing clients, which will keep them from the industry's horrific annual turnover.

Since everyone has some type of insurance, brokers should go down the Funnel and give prospects the ability to look at what they've got in place, what their current brokers may be able to help them with but have overlooked. If prospects realize they're missing something, they'd rather work within their current system and call their regular brokers. You need to ask questions like, "What would you need to know about working with me or my company that would make it possible for you to work with me to supplement your current coverage?"

Real Estate

Realtors show at least 50 percent more homes than they need to. They listen for a while to what buyers say they want and act immediately on superficial buying criteria. By putting prospects through the Buying Decision Funnel, realtors can gather the exact specifications and will only need to show a small number of homes. Realtors need to ask questions like, "What specifically do you need in order to buy? Name five things." And, "How would you know this is the exact house you want?" And, "What would you need from me to know you'd like to work with me?"

Office Peripherals

In this category—called business-to-business—I'm putting all the products and services that companies need in order to run the show: office equipment, hardware, software, paper goods, employees, training, management skills. I'm putting these together because they all share a common problem in that someone at some point has provided service in all these areas. As a potential new supplier, you must understand the present situation and then ask if there are any conditions under which the prospect will consider a supplementary solution or supplier.

Consumer Purchases

The business-to-consumer marketplace is currently dominated by telemarketing, which is the prime example of senders without receivers. Because telemarketing calls often take place at inconvenient times for prospects, lots of rapport is needed. It is imperative to say something like, "I know this might be dinner time. Is this inconvenient for you? Should I call back at a better time?" For some reason, telemarketers believe that if they ask questions like that, they will lose an opportunity to sell. If they don't ask, of course, they never had the opportunity anyway: they are using selling patterns, sending without a receiver, trying to sell a product with no buyer. ***People buy using their own buying patterns, not a seller's selling patterns.***

Multilevel Marketing (MLM)

Since there are two outcomes to MLM—selling the product and signing up new distributors—rapport and questioning are vital. I have been to several open evenings of this type of program and have found them all to be the same: here is why our product is good, here are some people who have been successful, and here is how much money you will make if you sign up *X,* then *XXX* people. They are almost like twelve-step programs, including motivational stories about how someone went from being a luggage handler with a failing marriage to working harmoniously *with* their spouse and earning $5,000 a month, in under a year. It is almost impossible to not feel their excitement and want it for yourself. But once you leave, it's cotton candy: a seller with potentially no receiver.

At a jewelry MLM program, I asked one of the motivators if she would address her statements to people's buying patterns rather than to what she was trying to sell. She stared at me for a few moments, smiled, then said, "We're all here to make money. What else is there?" So much for buying patterns.

When working with MLM, find out what prospects' interests are. Do they just want the product? The management scheme? Both? What is their timing, work situation, skill level? What would they need from you over time? What level of responsibility are they used to taking? Willing to take?

So much time is spent pitching success stories, assuming they'll convince. Don't waste your time if the people either just want the product or will be inappropriate associates.

Car Sales

Car salespeople seem to have the worst reputations. I don't know why. They are just doing what every other seller is doing: open, pitch, close.

When prospects come into a car dealership, the seller should first sit them down and go through the Funnel with them. After doing this, show them those cars that will meet their criteria:

color, price, size, features. How will they make a decision? How will they want to work with you to feel comfortable buying from you? How many other dealerships are they working with? What type of comparison shopping are they doing? How can you best support them?

It's not about what you have to sell, it's about what they need to buy, and who they will feel comfortable buying from.

Medical/Pharmaceutical/Third-Party Sales

This is an interesting sale, since the rep has almost no way of knowing who is buying what when the sale comes from a third party. It's like flying blind. You need lots of rapport and loyalty here, especially with nurses and receptionists. Use the Funnel with the ancillary staff: What suppliers are you using now? Do you ever add suppliers to your current relationships? What would you need to know about me or my company or product to be willing to add me to your roll? How would you know the doctor should take time to see me? The real "sale" here is to the screen. Doctors are willing to try most things once. The problem is time and brand loyalty. Find out how they buy.

Buying Facilitation on the Phone versus Face-to-Face

Because there is so much multinational business today, the telephone is being used more often for sales and follow-up. Traditionally, however, sales has been a face-to-face profession, with the phone being used only to get appointments. But making appointments with unqualified prospects, with people who haven't recognized their buying patterns, is a waste at least 80 percent of the time. (IBM estimates that each sales visit costs $379 in expenses and lost time.) It is amazing that with the dreadful success ratio of appointments, they continue to be such a highly accepted strategy.

Use the telephone to do your qualifying. Because of the level of rapport you establish with Buying Facilitation, people are delighted to go down the Funnel with you. Once they discover what they need and how they need it, they will move you to the next phase, *which may or may not be a face-to-face visit,* depending on their buying patterns.

When you begin your connection with a prospect based on your selling pattern of a face-to-face visit, you are disqualifying all prospective buyers who either are uncomfortable making an appointment with someone they don't know, or haven't recognized a specific need yet. You get people who are "comparison shopping," and therefore you are wasting your time.

Spend at least four hours a day, three days a week, on the phone, finding those prospects who qualify. Use the other two days as field days to visit the people who are qualified and wanting to see you in person as part of their buying pattern. There is no reason you shouldn't have a 90 percent closing ratio for your visits.

By the way, while on those visits, use the same approach as with the phone. Get into rapport, use the Buying Decision Funnel, and ask, agree, or summarize. Present or pitch according to the prospect's needs. The prospect will tell you how to go forward.

Doing It Is like Bungee Jumping

When you are first learning Buying Facilitation, it will be so different from what you have been used to that it may feel like you are totally out of control: your ego will be screaming, you won't be an expert any more, you won't be in control of closing, all your product knowledge may be wasted, you won't be a savior. But you will have a different type of control, and you will be able to sell more product, have happier clients, and have an easier day with little rejection. You'll spend less time in the field, more time qualifying on the phone, less time making presentations, less time writing proposals, more time learning how to listen and ask questions. And you will have sales, knowing you are finding those people who need your product and your collaboration.

It is different. But learning it is like learning anything else: you need to practice. It will be uncomfortable at first. But if you are wanting to realign your behaviors with your beliefs and sell from an ethical base, it's worth a shot.

Chapter 17

Reinventing Business By Reinventing Sales

As a way of taking vacations in conjunction with furthering my personal growth, I visit jungle habitats in remote areas of the world. I feel at home in jungles, where trees and flowers and plants all live in support of one another. And the people, the "Leavers" as Daniel Quinn calls them in *Ishmael*, are living a harmonious life with each other and with nature.

I feel such complete rest in the jungle: the powerlessness of my human condition is much in evidence and juxtaposed with the power I garner from my oneness with the people. Here it is okay for me to just be, with no expectations of how—so different from the doing of my normal life. I never realized the toll the American business culture takes on me until I sat alone in a forest for the first time. I didn't know it was possible to belong, to actually have a place in the world, without having to earn it.

I feel safe in the jungle. Life is simple. Among the indigenous people I am recognized as a contributing member of the group, with a heart that nourishes, hands that help, a back that carries, legs that travel. Each member does his or her share to support survival. There is no competition. The people living in the jungle are all part of a fabric, and when one thread is missing the garment is torn.

I am continually amazed at the ways the inhabitants all care for each other. In the Amazon, it is normal for a young monkey, whose mother has been killed for food, to hop onto a lactating dog, make a home on her back, and drink from her teats until the monkey is weaned. The "give and take" tree offers poisonous fluid on one end, while the other end offers a healing salve. Widows are taken in by brothers-in-law to be cared for and respected as new wives. Families all work together to build homes, to hunt and fish, to survive.

In Belize, frigate birds, whose beaks are relatively useless, live harmoniously alongside booby birds—facile hunters. The frigates steal the boobies' food and nesting materials, while the boobies good-naturedly chase them to retrieve the bounty. In water habitats, hermit crabs use other creatures' shells to live in, and pilot fish live under sharks and whales to clean them and receive protection in the bargain.

Diversity is a part of the structure. Each task, each adaptation, each iteration is supported by the whole, made richer by it, and defined by it.

We in the United States live lives of separateness. Those of us lucky enough to lead traditional, middle-class lives are faced with our narcissism, our loneliness, our fractured relationships. To alleviate the pain in our lives we have therapy, we go to twelve-step meetings, we find religions and ceremony. We spend $2 billion annually going to the movies. Two-thirds of all marriages end in divorce. It is estimated that 70 percent of us have jobs rather than doing our "work"—earning a paycheck rather than living our life's passion.

In modern business, our corporations have supported our separateness. Money, materialism, product elitism, consumption, competition have been the goals. The *Harvard Business Review* included an article by Alan Grant and Leonard Schlesinger in the September-October 1995 issue that stated: "Achieving the full profit potential of each customer relationship should be the fundamental goal of every business." Where are the people in this equation? Do people come to work just to support the profitability of their employer? What happens to people when they must leave their hearts and passions at home in order to go into work each day?

The profit motive worked for a while and is still obviously being espoused. But at what cost? Alienation; unhappy employees; underutilized potential; underproductive workplaces; undervaluation of the uniqueness of each thread in the fabric; and inability to weave the threads together, leaving us separate and in pain.

The Job without Which There Could Be No Business

But the old ways aren't working anymore. We are changing. Our corporations and their people are in chaos. We don't know where we are going, but we know we can't stay where we've been. We are facing vast cultural changes, complete with shifts in values, ethics, and expectations. No longer is it okay to put product first: people come first. No longer can our clients be expected to sit back and "take it." Both managers and employees are now asking to become empowered: to add their passion and brains and competencies into the weave, to work together as a whole. Managers no longer give directives: their new job is to support the team, to coach them, and to facilitate an environment that will bring forth their shared gifts.

But the new culture, the new ethics, have not touched the sales arena in any substantial way—not until now.

As the baseline of business, the sine qua non, the task without which there would be no business, sales has been the foundation upon which corporations have been built. Sales is the very essence of our materialistic world view.

It's time to bring our values into the sales arena. By supporting our customers in making the best decisions for themselves or their companies, we can work interdependently, with our hearts and passions and creativity *and* make more money selling more product than ever before. By facilitating our customers in discovering the best route for them to get their needs met, we empower our customers and ourselves. We must use our skills and expertise as salespeople to create an environment of collaboration in which both seller and buyer get their needs met for the highest good of both.

Until now, business has not had a selling strategy that could meet it in its places of transformation. Until now, businesses have been working on change while using manipulation strategies at the core level of promoting product.

Just Imagine

There no longer has to be an incongruity between values and behaviors. In fact, sales, as the pivotal function in each company, can now lead the way and support change.

When I enter a corporation to train sellers in this new way to sell, I am aware of the implications of the training. The sales force not only deals with outside clients, but comes into daily contact with the full range of internal clients company-wide: purchasing, accounting, management, customer service, manufacturing.

Imagine if sellers entered the sales profession using the same values and ethics with which we live our personal lives.

Imagine working in a profession that provides the foundation for all business to change.

Imagine sales departments that no longer have pushes at the end of the quarter to close business, and employ sellers who love coming to work, who have fun with their prospects, and who know they are making a difference in the world—every day.

Imagine a sales operating budget that decreases each year because sellers need to use travel expenses less as they learn to use the phone more effectively to qualify prospects, or a company that needs fewer salespeople because a smaller number of sellers brings in a larger share of the revenue.

Imagine a company that puts relationship first, so there's no longer a steel company, or a bank: just a customer service company that produces steel or provides banking services.

Imagine a corporation in which people take responsibility for creating a "We Space" in every interaction, in which people help each other discover how they can each get their needs met effectively and congruently, in which they know how to listen to each other—and people understand they are being heard.

Imagine a country in which each corporation promotes conscious communication, and expects people to learn the skills as part of their entry-level training.

Imagine a world in which each person has the skills to empower others, to offer direction and trust to help others discover their own answers.

Imagine.

Appendix

The Principles
and the Skills
of Buying Facilitation

The Principles:

1. You have nothing to sell if there's no one to buy.
2. Relationship comes first, task second.
3. The buyer has the answers; the seller has the questions.
4. Service is the goal; discovery is the outcome; a sale may be the solution.
5. People buy only when they can't fill their own needs.
6. People buy using their own buying patterns, not a seller's selling patterns.

The Skills:

Questioning
Formulating and asking Facilitative questions
Asking questions from structure to elicit content

Listening
System of navigation (Self, Observer, Neutral)
System of awareness (structure, content, meta-message)
System of delivery (sender, receiver)
Moving between communication choice points

Collaborating
Sender/receiver
"We Space"
Trust
Rapport

Buying Patterns
Recognizing them
Supporting them
Eliminating selling patterns

The Buying Decision Funnel

Goals:

- Support discovery of systemic problems and solutions.
- Sequentially organize the prospective buyer's thinking process.
- Uncover elements of the Problem Space.
- Serve through conscious communication.

The Process:

1. *Where are we now?* Look at the entire environment as it is in the Present.

2. *Where are we going?* Look at where the company is going in the Future, both short term and intermediate term.

3. *What internal resources are in place now?* Notice if all the components are in place to bring the company through to the Future vision.

4. *What specifically is missing that we need to get from here to there?* If there is a piece missing that would hinder the company from getting to the Future vision, the missing piece must be found and added.

5. *What resources do we have that might fix the problem?* Look around the environment again. Talk with the team and collaboratively search for ways to use current internal resources to supply the missing piece.

6. *At what point do we agree that what we've got isn't working well enough to solve our problem?* If there are no internal resources that will fix the problem, prepare to look externally for resources to supply the missing piece. Get team agreement and feedback on how to proceed.

7. *What are our criteria for choosing an external solution?* Determine with the team the criteria to be used to locate, choose, and integrate the missing piece. Look at the systemic issues to identify criteria (i.e., people and staffing needs, internal politics, timing, budget, outcomes).

8. *What are the possible solutions available and where do we find them?* Authorize team members to search for the missing piece by exploring potential external resources using the chosen criteria as a filter for choice.

9. *How do we know when it's time to bring in the new solution?* Find several potential fixes. Bring possibilities back to the environment and entire team to get consensus on the best choice.

10. *Purchase the solution.* Bring in the external fix. Integrate it into the existing environment.

Awareness for Conscious and Responsible Communication

The following types of information awareness are needed in order to ensure conscious and responsible communication:

Physical Environment—Relating to a prospect's Problem Space

The work environment, including sociopolitical issues

Current suppliers

Evidence that what is in place is working

Evidence that what is in place is not working

Budget

Personnel

Time frames

Hierarchy of criteria: quality, cost, time

Collaborative Environment—Relating to seller/prospect interaction

Are we in rapport? How do I know? Do we continue?

Do we have shared values?

Have I created a "We Space"? Are we working together?

Is there trust?

Am I getting the right level of information?

Personal Environment—Relating to seller's level of responsibility

Am I moving between Self and Observer?

Am I curious or manipulative?

Am I summarizing?

Am I entering into this person's reality sensitively?

Do I recognize the difference between the meta-message, the content, and the structure?

Am I facilitating discovery concerning political issues to be avoided or noted, and how am I supporting resolution?

Bibliography

Bosworth, Michael T. *Solution Selling: Creating Buyers in Difficult Selling Markets.* Chicago: Irwin Professional Publishing, 1995.

Carnegie, Dale. *How to Win Friends and Influence People.* New York: Pocket Books, 1936.

Chappell, Tom. *The Soul of a Business.* New York: Bantam Books, 1993.

DiCarlo, Russell E. *Towards a New World View: Conversations at the Leading Edge.* Erie, Pa.: Epic Publishing, 1996.

Dorsey, David. *The Force.* New York: Ballantine Books, 1994.

Grant, Alan W.H. and Leonard Schlesinger. "Realize your customer's full profit potential." *Harvard Business Review* (September-October 1995), 59.

Hawken, Paul. *The Ecology of Commerce.* New York: HarperBusiness, 1993.

Korten, David C. *When Corporations Rule the World.* West Hartford, Conn. and San Francisco, Calif.: Kumarian Press and Berrett-Koehler, 1995.

Miller, Robert B. and Stephen E. Heiman, with Tad Tuleja. *Strategic Selling: The Unique Sales System Proven Successful by America's Best Companies.* New York: William Morrow & Co., Inc., 1985.

Morgen, Sharon Drew. *Sales on the Line: Meeting the Business Demands of the '90s through Phone Partnering.* Portland, Ore.: Metamorphous Press, 1993.

Quinn, Daniel. *Ishmael.* New York: A Bantam/Turner Book, 1993.

Rackham, Neil. *SPIN Selling.* New York: McGraw-Hill Book Company, 1988.

Sandler Sales Institute. *Corporate Training and Development Program.* Audiocassette, 1993.

Schank, Roger C. *Tell Me a Story: A New Look at Real and Artificial Memory.* New York: Charles Scribner's, 1990.

Schank, Roger C., with Peter Childers. *The Creative Attitude: Learning to Ask and Answer the Right Questions.* New York: MacMillan, 1988.

Shook, Robert L. *The Greatest Sales Stories Ever Told: From the World's Best Salespeople.* New York: McGraw-Hill, Inc., 1995.

Shorris, Earl. *A Nation of Salesmen: The Tyranny of the Market and the Subversion of Culture.* New York: Avon Books, 1994.

Tarnas, Richard. *The Passion of the Western Mind: Understanding the Ideas That Have Shaped Our World View.* New York: Ballantine Books, 1991.

Werth, Jacques, and Nicholas E. Ruben. *High Probability Selling: Re-invents the Selling Process.* Newtown, Pa.: ABBA Publishing, 1992.

Wilson, Larry, with Hersch Wilson. *Changing the Game: The New Way to Sell.* New York: Fireside, a division of Simon and Schuster, 1987.

Wilson, Larry, with Hersch Wilson. *Stop Selling, Start Partnering: The New Thinking about Finding & Keeping Customers.* Vermont: Omneo, a division of Oliver Wight Publications, 1995.

Ziglar, Zig. *Ziglar on Selling: The Ultimate Handbook for the Complete Sales Professional of the Nineties.* New York: Ballantine Books, 1991.

Index

About the Author

Sharon Drew Morgen has been in sales for 17 years following a 13-year career as social worker and probation officer for the City of New York.

Sharon Drew attended Syracuse University School of Journalism and graduated from the University of Connecticut with a degree in English/Journalism. She did graduate work in Health Sciences at the City University of New York, while working with the Department of Social Services and raising a child. As part of her thesis, she began a Parenting program for parents of schizophrenic children. That program is still in operation in New York City.

Following her graduate work, Sharon Drew became a stockbroker on Wall Street. Between 1979 and 1984, she worked with Merrill Lynch, Kidder Peabody, and EFHutton. It was on Wall Street that Sharon Drew learned then-current sales techniques.

In 1984, Sharon Drew used her sales experience to take on a start-up computer support operation in London, England. During the beginning phase of this job, she developed Buying Facilitation, and using this new sales approach, grew her one-woman operation into a $5,000,000 business with 43 employees in only 4 years.

When Sharon Drew decided to leave the computer support company in 1988, her clients began calling, asking her to teach her new sales technology to their salespeople. Since she had never trained or developed sales training programs, she traveled in the United States and the United Kingdom taking sales training programs to learn how it was done. She discovered that sales trainers trained the way sellers sold, believing they had something to impart and the audience had to accept what the trainer thought they needed to learn. Sharon Drew then designed a new training method which assumes the learners have the answers—just as the buyer does—giving the trainers the job of supporting the learners in uncovering their own information.

After conducting sales training for a year in London for companies such as British Telecom, GE Information Services, and DEC, she took a sabbatical, and moved back to the United States to a ranch in Taos, New Mexico. During the sabbatical, she realized the importance of her new sales technology. Given her profound belief in people and the strength of collaboration, she felt obliged to make this new approach to selling, which she named Buying Facilitation, widely available. She then wrote *Sales on the Line*, published in 1993, to introduce Buying Facilitation, and went on the road again to facilitate the learning of the new sales paradigm in American business. In 1994, Sharon Drew published a cartoon book, *SOMEBODY Makes a Difference*, about intuition and collaboration among group members.

Sharon Drew's dream is to have Buying Facilitation used by every salesperson in the world, replacing the standard sales approaches. As evidence that the new sales paradigm is being welcomed into corporate America, her clients have included IBM, Union Bank of California, Bethlehem Steel, DEC, Whirlpool Financial, Boston Scientific, and Dean Witter Reynolds.

Sharon Drew has been on a life mission to heal communications in the world, spending much time on a personal journey of discovery and recovery. Toward this end, she spent many years studying NeuroLinguistic Programming with the founders of the field to assist her in understanding communication and personal choice in communication patterns. To heal her spirit, she has traveled around the world during the last few years, studying with shamans, healers, and sages.

In 1985, during her time in London, Sharon Drew founded the Dystonia Society, a non-profit organization to raise funds and awareness to help people like her son, George who suffer with the disabling family of neurological diseases called dystonia. Currently the Dystonia Society operates in six countries, has over 5,000 members, and has assisted dozens of children to walk again.

Sharon drew has also developed a model for conscious choice in communication and is working on a new book which will teach people how to consciously choose the communication that most effectively serves understanding. This model can be used in education, negotiation, management, and in personal and family relationships.

Sharon Drew speaks on and teaches the following programs: *The New Paradigm in Sales*, *Managing the Buying Facilitation Environment*, *Sales on the Line (telephone sales)*, *Choosing to Serve Customers*, *Creativity in Business*, *Intuition in the Workplace*, *The Tools of Conscious Choice*, and *Consciousness in Business*.

Should you wish to attend seminars on any of the topics listed above, or to create an in-house program in Buying Facilitation, please contact:

Morgen Facilitations, Inc.	Phone: (505) 776-2509
Box 1926	Fax: (505) 776-2119
Taos, NM 87571	Email: sdmorgen@Rt66.com

Note: Morgen Facilitations, Inc. can customize in-house programs in Buying Facilitation for any environment. They offer trainer-training and licensing agreements to support in-house training. *Please note that specific skills are needed to teach this approach.*

Berrett-Koehler Publishers

ERRETT-KOEHLER is an independent publisher of books, periodicals, and other publications at the leading edge of new thinking and innovative practice on work, business, management, leadership, stewardship, career development, human resources, entrepreneurship, and global sustainability.

Since the company's founding in 1992, we have been committed to supporting the movement toward a more enlightened world of work by publishing books, periodicals, and other publications that help us to integrate our values with our work and work lives, and to create more humane and effective organizations.

We have chosen to focus on the areas of work, business, and organizations, because these are central elements in many people's lives today. Furthermore, the work world is going through tumultuous changes, from the decline of job security to the rise of new structures for organizing people and work. We believe that change is needed at all levels—individual, organizational, community, and global—and our publications address each of these levels.

We seek to create new lenses for understanding organizations, to legitimize topics that people care deeply about but that current business orthodoxy censors or considers secondary to bottom-line concerns, and to uncover new meaning, means, and ends for our work and work lives.

See next page for other books from Berrett-Koehler Publishers

Other leading-edge business books from Berrett-Koehler Publishers

Customers As Partners
Building Relationships That Last
Chip R. Bell

WRITTEN WITH PASSION and humor, this groundbreaking work provides step-by-step guidelines for enhancing long-term customer loyalty and achieving lasting success. Chip Bell offers insights on how to keep the quality of customer relationships central in every interaction by creating sustaining personal bonds—the true source of profitability.

Paperback, 256 pages, 1/96 • ISBN 1-881052-78-8 CIP • **Item no. 52788-171 $15.95**

Hardcover 9/94 • ISBN 1-881052-54-0 CIP • **Item no. 52540-171 $24.95**

Managing By Values

Ken Blanchard and Michael O'Connor

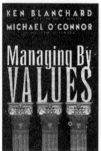

BASED ON over twenty-five years of research and application, *Managing by Values* provides a practical game plan for defining, clarifying, and communicating an organization's values and aligning its practices throughout the organization. While previous books have addressed the importance of values, *Managing by Values* provides a clear methodology for defining and implementing such values to achieve organizational, group, team, and individual objectives.

Hardcover, 140 pages, 1/97 • ISBN 1-57675-007-8 CIP
Item no. 50078-171 $20.00

A Higher Standard of Leadership
Lessons from the Life of Gandhi

Keshavan Nair

THIS IS THE FIRST BOOK to apply lessons from Gandhi's life to the practical tasks faced by today's business and political leaders. Through illustrative examples from Gandhi's life and writings, Keshavan Nair explores the process of making decisions, setting goals, and implementing actions in the spirit of service that is essential to the realization of a higher standard of leadership in our workplaces and communities.

Paperback, 174 pages, 1/97 • ISBN 1-57675-011-6 CIP
Item no. 50116-171 $16.95

Available at your favorite bookstore, or call (800) 929-2929

Artful Work

Awakening Joy, Meaning, and Commitment in the Workplace

Dick Richards

DICK RICHARDS applies the assumptions of artists about work and life to the challenges facing people and organizations in today's rapidly changing world. He reminds us that all work can be artful, and that artfulness is the key to passion and commitment. Readers will learn to take an inspired approach to their work, renewing their experience of it as a creative, participative, and purposeful endeavor.

Hardcover, 144 pages, 3/95 • ISBN 1-881052-63-X CIP
Item no. 5263X-171 $25.00

Repacking Your Bags

Lighten Your Load for the Rest of Your Life

Richard J. Leider and David A. Shapiro

LEARN HOW to climb out from under the many burdens you're carrying and find the fulfillment that's missing in your life. A simple yet elegant process teaches you to balance the demands of work, love, and place in order to create and live your own vision of success.

Paperback, 234 pages, 2/96 • ISBN 1-881052-87-7 CIP
Item no. 52877-171 $14.95

Hardcover, 1/95 • ISBN 1-881052-67-2 CIP
Item no. 52672-171 $21.95

Your Signature Path

Gaining New Perspectives on Life and Work

Geoffrey M. Bellman

Your Signature Path explores the uniqueness of the mark each of us makes in the world. Bestselling author Geoffrey M. Bellman offers thought-provoking insights and practical tools for evaluating who you are, what you are doing, and where you want your path to lead.

Hardcover, 200 pages, 10/96 • ISBN 1-57675-004-3 CIP
Item no. 50043-171 $24.95

Managers As Mentors
Building Partnerships for Learning
Chip R. Bell

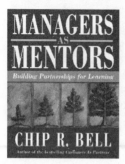

MANAGERS AS MENTORS is a provocative guide to helping associates grow and adapt in today's tumultuous organizations. Chip Bell persuasively shows that mentoring means valuing creativity over control, fostering growth by facilitating learning, and helping others get smart, not just get ahead. His hands-on, down-to-earth advice takes the mystery out of effective mentoring, teaching leaders to be the confident coaches integral to learning organizations.

Hardcover, 206 pages, 6/96 • ISBN 1-881052-92-3 CIP
Item no. 52923-171 $24.95

A Complaint Is a Gift
Using Customer Feedback As a Strategic Tool
Janelle Barlow and Claus Møller

A COMPLAINT IS A GIFT is a "how-to" book for those who want to turn complaints into a strategic tool to increase business and customer satisfaction. Presenting dozens of real-life striking examples of poor—and excellent—complaint handling, Barlow and Møller show that companies must view complaints as gifts if they are to have loyal customers.

Paperback, 232 pages, 3/96 • ISBN 1-881052-81-8 CIP
Item no. 52818-171 $16.95

Tyranny of the Bottom Line
Why Corporations Make Good People Do Bad Things
Ralph Estes

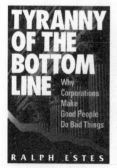

HERE IS the story of corporate power gone awry—bringing injury and death to employees, financial and personal loss to customers, desolation to communities, pollution and hazardous waste to the nation. Emphasizing the notion that all of us are stakeholders in the large corporation—with an investment, an interest in its performance, and a right to accountability—Ralph Estes provides a practical, specific plan for creating more effective and humane companies, restoring the original public purpose of the corporate system, and allowing managers to make choices that effectively and ethically balance the interests of everyone.

Hardcover, 310 pages, 1/96 • ISBN 1-881052-75-3 CIP • **Item no. 52753-171**
$27.95

Available at your favorite bookstore, or call (800) 929-2929